D0862637

Praise for . . . *Telling the Tale*

Elie Wiesel is one of the great people of our times — not just because he survived when millions did not, but because he brought their message, and his own, to our minds and hearts. Harry James Cargas has produced a fine memory book, a *Festschrift*, for Elie's 65th birthday. May Elie have many more birthdays and continue to be a light in the darkness.

> — Rev. Theodore M. Hesburgh, C.S.C.,
> President Emeritus, University of Notre Dame

For 35 years Wiesel has been credited and criticized for writing on behalf of Holocaust victims and survivors. His legacy, however, will depend less on his chosen mission "to bear witness" than on his enabling talents to more than fulfill that mission. We are grateful, then, for this volume. Its impressive range of essays, interviews, reflections, and poems captures a luminous Wiesel yearning for answers while doubting — always doubting — that there are any.

> — Dr. Dennis B. Klein, Director, Braun Center for Holocaust
> Studies, Anti-Defamation League of B'nai B'rith

This book speaks directly to those whose souls and lives have been forever changed by *Night* and subsequent work. For those of us who devote our lives to studying and teaching about the *Shoah*, we can never learn enough about Elie Wiesel or have adequate time and exposure to the full depth of his wisdom — his words — his mysticism — his magical effect. The abundance of love and admiration expressed in this volume by scholars, physicians and poets from around the world provides a fitting tribute to the teacher of us all.

> — Dr. Marcia Sachs Littell, Director, The Philadelphia Center
> on the Holocaust, Genocide and Human Rights

Over the years, Professor Cargas has performed a unique service as chronicler of the intellectual journey of Nobel Laureate Wiesel. This volume, prepared in honour of Wiesel's 65th birthday, adds another important contribution to the literature on both the Holocaust and its principal voice. Many of the best known names in the field offer moving tributes to one who has been rightly termed "America's best known Jewish author." This is a volume to be eagerly added to one's shelf.

> — Dr. Hubert G. Locke, Professor, University of Washington,
> and Vice-President, Annual Scholars Conference on the
> Holocaust

Telling the Tale captures both Wiesel and Cargas at their very best. The volume gives us new glimpses into the complex personality of Wiesel, thanks in large part to the masterful interviewing ability of Cargas. Bob Costas further expands our understanding of Wiesel — the man, the survivor, the seeker of God and contemporary justice. The interpretive essays by the likes of Littell, Soelle, Berger and Roth offer the reader a wide range of reactions to Wiesel's writings and reveal the broad impact of his thought. The volume is clearly both a fine tribute to Wiesel on his 65th birthday and an excellent introduction to a literary career of more than three decades' duration.

> — Dr. John T. Pawlikowski, Professor, Catholic
> Theological Union, and Member, Executive Committee,
> U.S. Holocaust Memorial Council

Telling the Tale: A Tribute to Elie Wiesel is a volume which demands of its reader the most intense scrutinization possible. One does not enter Elie Wiesel's world easily. It is a world made up of many questions and few answers; it is a world that allows the outsider to glimpse only that which Elie Wiesel wishes him or her to see. Not that Wiesel is trying to protect some secret pocket of knowledge. If only it were that simple. When you have looked over the abyss and have lived in the universe of the Holocaust Kingdom, you must remain silent in certain matters, because you need to protect those who have not looked over the edge, who have not lived in your universe. They cannot, nor should they expect to, know what Wiesel knows; they cannot, nor should they expect to, imagine what he has imagined.

Readers of this volume should know that in Wiesel's words and in the words of those who try to understand what he writes and what he believes, they are reading the authentic voice of a survivor, the voice that in the immediate days and months after the liberation called for a revolution in Jewish and world history. The fervor of those days lives on in Elie Wiesel, in his words and in his deeds.

> — Dr. Abraham J. Peck, Director, American Jewish Archives

Telling the Tale is Harry James Cargas' labor of love and creativity in honor of Elie Wiesel. Once again, we hear Wiesel's witness for the dead and the living. More than ever, we need to listen to it.

> — Dr. Carol Rittner, R.S.M., Editor of *Beyond the Diary: Anne
> Frank and the World*

Elie Wiesel bears Jewish witness for our time, teaching how universal meaning emerges from an all-embracing confrontation with the singularity of one's experience. In this splendidly evocative anthology, his Christian friend Harry James Cargas illustrates just how fertile and essential this testimony is for us all as we adjust to the eternal shadow of human and divine apostasy in our century.

— Pierre Sauvage, President and Founder of Friends of Le Chambon and producer, director, and writer of *Weapons of the Spirit*

As editor and contributor to *Telling the Tale: A Tribute to Elie Wiesel*, Harry James Cargas has once more added an important and timely volume to the Holocaust literature. Through poetry and prose, this book offers valuable insights into Elie Wiesel, the man, as it adds to our understandings and feelings about a wide range of moral and philosophical issues that touch on the Nazi destruction of European Jews. With a skillful editorial hand, Cargas has succeeded in assembling a rich variety of materials, making this book a provocative and important invitation for thoughts and emotions.

— Dr. Nechama Tec, Professor, University of Connecticut, and author of *Defiance: The Bielski Partisans*

"Remembrance leads to Redemption while Forgetfulness leads to Exile." These words confront the visitor as he/she leaves *Yad Vashem*, the memorial in Jerusalem built in remembrance of six million Jews who died in the Holocaust. *Telling the Tale*, written in a well-deserved tribute to Elie Wiesel, takes the reader on a journey of remembrance of this attempted annihilation of Jews just because they were Jews. All of us owe a debt of gratitude to each and every survivor of the *Shoah* — especially to Elie Wiesel.

Author, philosopher, poet, teacher, Elie Wiesel, through his writings, lectures, TV and radio interviews has charged each of his readers/listeners to *care*. Never again can any of his students be indifferent, apathetic to what is happening anywhere in this world such as in Crown Heights, New York, or the former Yugoslavia. It is Elie Wiesel who has helped me see that in "every protest there is a spark of Divine." It is he who challenges me daily to try to come to grips with the Holocaust.

Telling the Tale is truly a tribute to our friend and teacher, Elie Wiesel. Congratulations on your 65th birthday, Elie, and to all who honored you in this special volume, thus making it possible for you to continue to "Tell the Tale."

— Dr. Rose Thering, O.P., Executive Director, National Christian Leadership Conference for Israel

TELLING THE TALE

A TRIBUTE TO

ELIE WIESEL

TELLING THE TALE

A TRIBUTE TO

ELIE WIESEL

ON THE OCCASION OF
HIS 65TH BIRTHDAY
ESSAYS, REFLECTIONS, AND POEMS

EDITED BY

HARRY JAMES CARGAS

TIME BEING BOOKS
POETRY IN SIGHT AND SOUND

Time Being Books
10411 Clayton Road
Saint Louis, Missouri 63131

Time Being Books is an imprint of Time Being Press, Inc.
Saint Louis, Missouri

Time Being Books volumes are printed on acid-free paper, and binding materials are chosen for strength and durability.

Library of Congress Cataloging-in-Publication Data

Telling the tale : a tribute to Elie Wiesel on the occasion of his
  65th birthday : essays, reflections, and poems / edited by Harry
  James Cargas. — 1st ed.
     p.   cm.
  Includes bibliographical references.
  ISBN 1-56809-006-4 (cloth) — ISBN 1-56809-007-2 (pbk.)
  1. Wiesel, Elie, 1928- . 2. Authors, French — 20th century.
  3. Holocaust, Jewish (1939-1945) — Influence.   I. Wiesel, Elie.
  1928- . II. Cargas, Harry J.
  PQ36.W54T45 1993
  813'.54 — dc20   93-27376
                                             C I P

Cover design by Tony Tharenos and Kathryn McDaniel Smith
Book design and typesetting by Lori Loesche
Manufactured in the United States of America

First Edition, first printing (October 1993)

74984

Acknowledgments

The editor wishes particularly to thank Jerry Call and Lori Loesche, Senior Editor and Editor, respectively, of Time Being Books for their efforts and dedication in making this volume a reality. Also deserving gratitude for proofreading the final manuscript are Sheri Vandermolen and Trilogy Brodsky.

I am extremely grateful to all the contributors for permission to use their work in this tribute. Finally, to NBC-TV, for enabling us to include the interview of Elie Wiesel done by Bob Costas on *LATER . . . with Bob Costas* and for permitting us to publish Gail M. Gendler's synopsis as an overview to this volume, I express my deep appreciation.

H.J.C.

CONTENTS

TELLING THE TALE

A TRIBUTE TO

ELIE WIESEL

An Interview with Elie Wiesel

by HARRY JAMES CARGAS

HJC: With another birthday it seems appropriate, natural, to reflect on time. What does time mean to you as it passes, gets further away from the Event?

EW: I am not afraid of time. Time to me is a puzzle. It is a vehicle, and I may choose to travel in it, or I may choose to run after it. As for the past in itself, strangely — maybe it's not so strange — I think about it now more often than then. With every day that passes, I dream about those days and nights more frequently. In a peculiar way the events that I dream about seem more brutal — more and more tragic. I see people with more clarity than before because now they involve not only the past but the present as well. In my dreams I see persons who are here and who were never there, yet I see them somehow involved with the people who were there. It is not so peculiar on one hand because writing is precisely that. I wrote *Night* because I wanted people who were not part of that period to feel something about that period. Maybe because I feel that even where I have not succeeded — I mean in books — I succeed in my dreams. And my readers, my anonymous readers, whom I know, I see them there.

HJC: In this journey that you are making, you have the vocation (not career or job) of teacher.

EW: Oh yes. I am rereading now and writing my memoirs. I came across something when I was in my mid-teens. We were a little group of young students. We held our services and had our lessons together. I remember the first time I gave a lecture. I remember I was both excited and terrified. It was after the war in the children's home (there were a hundred children there). We decided to have cultural evenings. My lecture was followed by a discussion. The theme: Is the ghetto good or bad for the Jewish people? There were

This previously unpublished interview, completed on June 25, 1991, is printed by permission of the author.

times when the ghetto was good. It created a spiritual atmosphere; the pressure was important for scholarship to grow.

HJC: Even a protective zone at times.

EW: Exactly. Therefore, I felt then as a teacher. Not only do I enjoy it, I like it so much that I don't take sabbaticals. I need my students, I love my students.

HJC: One of the things that concerns me is this: people lay a lot of grief onto you. People in jail. I've been here in your apartment twice when you were telephoned about survivors committing suicide — survivors whom you didn't even know. And much, much more. On whom do you lay your grief? How do you lay off *your* grief?

EW: I don't. I think I am strong enough — for the moment yet — to bear it. I choose writing. I hide it in my writing. If I were to stop working I would need somebody else to share it with. But I remain secretive about these things. First of all because I believe that what I really want to say I haven't begun saying yet. I know that what I have to say, what I will say, has not been said yet. In my memoirs I see things I haven't said yet. I would clarify certain matters, certain aims, and I may write the real story. One day, one day . . .

HJC: So my question is better *how* than *who*.

EW: Yes. It is writing. I am a Hassid. I don't have a *rebbe* now, I don't have a teacher, a master. If I had a master, I would go to see him. But all my masters are gone, so I speak to the dead quite a lot. And I write to the dead quite a lot. Whatever I cannot say to the reader, I say to them. It doesn't help much, but I do it nevertheless.

HJC: Specific dead?

EW: Specific dead, of course. Those that I knew. And those I did not. I feel their presence.

HJC: Why do you dance and sing?

EW: What is the alternative? We all have options. After the war most of the survivors did not share my obsession. Many wanted to live normal lives, to raise a family, to live comfortably — some even became wealthy. All they wanted was what they felt they deserved, what the world had taken away from them. Also they felt that with money they could do certain things. During the war, with money you could buy another day — a visa, a way to go to Spain or Switzerland. Money was important, so there was a kind of frenzy for years and years. They did what they felt was right. Some of us, very few, looked in another direction. We were attracted to study, to teaching and to knowledge, and to understanding, sharing, writing, and so forth. And to preserve the memory. Why did I reject the possibility of amassing wealth? I'm a bad businessman, but I could have tried my luck. Instead — very few people know this; I don't speak about it to people, not even you — I suffered from hunger many, many years after the war — even in New York. When I came to New York I worked for an Israeli paper, *Yedidot Achronot*, which paid me $200 a month. This sum covered my hotel, travel, laundry. Days passed without bread in my mouth. In the richest Jewish city in the world. True, people didn't know because I never complained, I never told anybody. I think about it now because I've run across it in my diary. Do you know that I would go to the UN bathroom, and I would take pieces of soap and bring them back to my hotel? I did not have enough money to buy soap. At the same time some survivors made millions of dollars. Was that then the alternative, making money? Or moving toward despair? Or becoming mad? Or choosing violence? My ability was limited. I had only one, this one: learning, writing, teaching. I had no other choice. This is my life. This is my temper, my mentality. I was meant for nothing else but to use words — either spoken or written. The subject changed, but the method remained the same. And the subject wasn't chosen, it was imposed upon me. Can you imagine: to live through such events and then reduce them to money? That's why I was never wealthy. I don't have much money. I don't feel attracted to it. I could have gone to Palestine then Israel, become a journalist probably. So what? I would have done the same thing. I would at some point, even then, have chosen to start writing. Or to become a teacher. Same thing again. Teaching and writing: for me there was nothing else I could do. That is why, as most of my characters, I choose dancing and singing in order not to yield to what is the opposite of singing and dancing. What is the opposite? Meanness, bitterness, and selfishness.

HJC: Is there a kind of defiance here?

EW: My answer — not to the Holocaust but to the options that presented themselves *after* the Holocaust — is something.

HJC: Well, there is a world that is glad that you are doing what you are doing.

ELIE WIESEL:
A BIOGRAPHICAL OVERVIEW

by GAIL M. GENDLER

As America's best known Jewish author, "the spiritual archivist of the Holocaust," Elie Wiesel's simmple, profound, humanitarian ideas reach out to the world. Wiesel says he "is here as a witness . . . not for the sake of the dead but for future generations . . . being a witness moves [me] to write, teach and speak." Wiesel has faced the choice between life and death, of succumbing to torture or of living through the inhumanities of the world. He continually chooses life; in doing so he fights to keep alive the memory of those who have perished. And through his writings, the future generations of Jews will be reminded of their past and be able to keep these memories, however painful, alive.

Since the publication of his first book, *Night*, in 1958, Wiesel has made Holocaust literature a part of our culture. He has brought to the world the horrors he and millions of other innocent men, women and children experienced in the concentration camps. Wiesel's childhood was taken from him in the camps. He says, "The child that I was, had been consumed in the flames. There remained only a shape that looked like me. A dark flame had entered into my soul and devoured it." *Night* has been called the most influential book confronting the genocide of the Jews.

Wiesel is credited with making the plight of the oppressed Soviet Jews a public issue. He reported on their oppression in *The Jews of Silence*, a recollection of his first visit to the USSR in 1965.

President Ronald Reagan presented the Congressional Gold Medal of Achievement to Wiesel in 1985. Wiesel's acceptance of the award gave him a public forum for his stern resentment of Reagan's scheduled visit to Bitburg, West Germany. Wiesel pleaded with

This synopsis (here in edited form) was prepared between September 22 and October 20, 1991, for Bob Costas by Gail M. Gendler of NBC-TV prior to Mr. Costas' interview with Elie Wiesel, the text of which appears on pp. 137-163.

Reagan to acknowledge both the American and Jewish victims of Nazism and to stand by them rather than align himself with their murderers.

Wiesel is a 1986 Nobel Peace Prize winner recognized for his work as a spokesman for world suffering. His philosophy can be defined by his statement, "Indifference is the greatest source of evil and danger to the world . . . indifference is the enemy."

Wiesel's name is associated with his mission in life "to bear witness." Wiesel has recognized suffering in Vietnam, Bangladesh, South America and Russia, and he has visited many areas of suffering around the world, such as Nicaragua, where he sought out the Miskito Indians to hear firsthand of their torture under the Sandinistas.

Wiesel was also involved with the panel discussion following *The Day After*, a television movie, seen by a huge audience, which dealt with the aftermath of a nuclear war. After seeing the program, Wiesel said he saw the whole world become Jewish as he witnessed the capricious behavior of man and the uncertainty after the destruction.

Today, fanaticism around the world and the fear that the century is going too fast concern Wiesel. He has said that twenty years ago, computers took up entire floors of buildings, and today we carry computers in our pockets. What may happen twenty years from now frightens him.

WIESEL'S BACKGROUND

Eliezer Wiesel was born on September 30, 1928, in Sighet, Romania. Sighet, a small village in the Carpathian Mountains, was ceded to Hungary in 1940 under German pressure but returned five years later to Romanian rule.

His parents, Shlomo and Sarah Feig Wiesel, brought to Elie's life a mixture of traditional Jewish, Talmudic thought and classic German philosophy. Shlomo, a shopkeeper, encouraged his son to learn modern Hebrew and its literature (rather than Biblical Hebrew) as well as Freud. Sarah urged her son's traditional Jewish studies and introduced the kabbalah (Jewish mysticism), Goethe and Schiller to him. Wiesel's life was study, his only distractions being chess and the violin. In the camps, he would play chess with other inmates without a board. They would play by memory. To this day, he still plays chess alone, a reminder of his childhood.

Wiesel found a great source of inspiration in his maternal grand-father, Dodye Feig. He lived in a village seven kilometers away, and his visits were always an occasion for Elie to celebrate. Dodye Feig was a farmer who shared his love of the Hasidic masters with his grandson, charming the boy with tales of these charismatic, evangelistic figures. Another childhood inspiration was the maggidim — the wandering storytellers. These men traveled from village to village, telling stories of the "outside" — other cultures, images and people. Both the maggidim and the Hasidic masters turn up in Wiesel's work.

To Elie and his three sisters, life in Sighet was dominated by the Jewish holidays and the Jewish Sabbath. But life changed drastically during the Passover holiday in the spring of 1944 with the arrival of the Germans. Wiesel writes about this experience in *Night*. He saw the Jewish leaders of his community arrested, a curfew imposed, homes ransacked, Jews forced to wear yellow stars, ghettos built and, finally, the deportation of all of Sighet's 15,000 Jews.

Auschwitz was the first stop for the Jews of Sighet. It was here that Wiesel's mother and youngest sister, Tzipora, perished. He was also separated here from his two other sisters, Hilda and Batya, both of whom survived the camps. Elie stayed by his father's side through four concentration camps: Birkenau, Auschwitz, Buna, and Buchenwald.

With "A-7713" tattooed onto his left arm, he became just a number in the Final Solution. From Auschwitz, Wiesel and his father were forced to march to Buna. There, along with 10,000 other inmates, he witnessed the hanging of a young boy for being an accomplice to an act of sabotage in the camp. He survived the infamous selection process by the brutal Dr. Joseph Mengele along with the continuous, round-the-clock killings of those condemned to death by Hitler. In Buna, Wiesel smelled burning flesh and watched man turn into animal in order to survive.

As the Russians advanced, the camp population marched to Gleiwitz. After three days there, Wiesel, his father and 100 other inmates boarded an open cattle car and traveled, in the cold winter, for ten days. Wiesel and his father were among the twelve to survive the trip to Buchenwald.

At Buchenwald, Shlomo Wiesel succumbed to starvation and beatings on January 28, 1945. Less than three months later, on April

11, 1945, the Americans liberated the camp. The Holocaust had ended, but Wiesel had experienced an emotional death.

At *Yad Vashem*, the Holocaust Memorial Museum in Jerusalem, one can see what Wiesel looked like at liberation. There is a life-size photo of a row of men lying in a bunk. They are gaunt, pale men wearing striped uniforms, staring vacantly out at the liberators. In the photo is Wiesel. When he looked into a mirror after liberation, he once said, "From the depths of the mirror, a corpse gazed back at me."

Following his liberation, the Americans asked Wiesel if he wanted to go home. But in Sighet, there was nothing. So the 16-year-old Wiesel boarded a train with 400 other Jewish orphans to Belgium. General Charles DeGaulle offered shelter to the children, and the train was redirected to France. In Normandy, Wiesel was placed in an orphanage under the supervision of a Jewish children's aid organization.

He was reunited with his two sisters after the elder one saw a photo of the orphans and recognized Elie. She contacted the orphanage director and made arrangements for Elie to travel to Paris. After their reunion, Elie returned to the care of the orphanage, where he continued his religious studies and became a choir director.

Wiesel moved to Paris in 1948 and spent the next three years studying literature, philosophy and psychology at the Sorbonne. He found employment in Paris as a choir director, a Hebrew and Bible teacher, and a translator and writer for a Yiddish paper. Wiesel's studies introduced him to the French existentialist writers. He identified with Camus and Sartre, copying their broad roles by eventually becoming a novelist, a speaker, an essayist and a moralist.

Wiesel began work as a journalist in 1948 as a correspondent for the French paper *L'Arche*. He was sent to Israel to cover the founding of the state. He stayed there for almost five months. He returned to France to become the Paris correspondent for Israel's *Yedidot Achronot*.

1954 was another turning point in Wiesel's life. It was then that he interviewed the French Roman Catholic writer and Nobel laureate, Francois Mauriac, for *Yedidot Achronot*. While Mauriac spoke about his secondhand knowledge of the deportation of Jewish children during the war, Wiesel looked at him, saying, "How often I've thought about the children . . . I was one of them." Mauriac eventually persuaded Wiesel to write. Mauriac provided the introduction to *Night* when it was published.

In 1956, Wiesel visited New York for *Yedidot Achronot* to cover the United Nations. He was in a terrible car accident soon after he arrived. He was hit by a cab on 46th Street and was thrown nearly a block; the ambulance picked him up on 45th Street. The first hospital the ambulance drove to refused to admit Wiesel for two reasons: his physical state was seemingly beyond repair, and he had refugee papers. He ended up at New York Hospital under the care of Dr. Paul Braunstein.

Wiesel was comatose for several days. Braunstein, an orthopedist, put Wiesel's broken body back together. He credits Braunstein with bringing him back to life. Wiesel spent nearly a year in a wheelchair following the accident. During this time, he decided to apply for United States citizenship, which he received in 1963. He began working for *The Jewish Daily Forward*, a Yiddish paper published in Manhattan's Lower East Side.

In 1958, Wiesel's first Holocaust work arrived with the publication in France of *Night*. It took an additional year for Wiesel's agent to find an American publisher for the book. In 1959, Hill & Wang purchased the manuscript for $100. It sold 1,046 copies in its first eighteen months on the market. Today it has sold over one million copies and is regarded as the most widely read work of Holocaust literature.

In 1964, Wiesel went back to Sighet. His account is detailed in the narrative *The Last Return*. For him, the Holocaust destroyed his birthplace. In Sighet, "Jews Street" had become "Street of the Deported." He searched the yard of his childhood home and unearthed a gift from his bar mitzvah. It was a watch he had buried there before deportation. The watch was eaten away, full of bugs and unrecognizable. The discovery put an end to his association with Sighet. He says, "I wanted to enter one last time and leave there all I possess, my memory."

In 1969, Wiesel married Marion Rose in Jerusalem, and in 1972, his son, Shlomo Elisha, was born. In a way, Shlomo Elisha's birth was a simple declaration and testimony to the survival of future generations of Jews. Finally, Wiesel had faith in the world and in mankind. Shlomo Elisha is named for his paternal grandfather, Shlomo; his second name is Hebrew for "God is salvation."

SOVIET JEWRY

In 1965, Wiesel made his first of many trips to Russia. His first trip was during the Jewish High Holidays (Rosh Hashanah and Yom Kippur), and he stayed through the holidays of Simchat Torah and Sukkot. In 1966, he published his reflections of his visit in *The Jews of Silence.*

This trip took Wiesel to Kiev, Moscow, Leningrad, Tbilisi and Kotaisi. He encountered scared, fearful Soviet Jews. Most of his meetings were with people who refused to offer their names but provided insight to the discrimination the Soviet Jews felt daily. Soviet Jews felt a total sense of isolation from their brethren and pounded Wiesel with questions testing the veracity of rumors regarding Israel and Jewish communities abroad. They told Wiesel of their distrust of Jewish informers.

During his stay, Wiesel witnessed the incredible emotion and joy the Soviet Jews felt when they celebrated the holiday of Simchat Torah, the festival of the giving of the Bible. He was in Moscow for the celebrations, where thousands of young and old Jews crowded the main synagogue and flooded the streets, dancing and singing for hours.

He saw the Soviet reverence for the members of the Israeli diplomatic corps. The Soviets would sing the Israeli national anthem spontaneously at Jewish ceremonies and looked to Israel as a symbol of Jewish strength. He also saw Hasidim — fervently religious Jews — who maintained their rituals and customs no matter what the price they paid in their work or social environments.

Wiesel visited Kiev in search of Babi Yar. There, in September 1941, the Nazis massacred 100,000 Soviet Jews and buried them in mass graves. Not knowing who could take him there, Wiesel paid a cabdriver to drive to Babi Yar. He took Wiesel to a place outside central Kiev, to an empty field.

He returned to the cab and asked to go back to the city. The driver looked at him laughingly, as if he were teasing Wiesel. Wiesel realized there was no way of knowing whether or not he was really at Babi Yar. "There is nothing to see at Babi Yar," Wiesel said. He realized that without a location marker, Babi Yar could be anywhere. The Jews were systematically killed while the world, and the Soviets, stood by in silence. Again, Wiesel knew that he must stand up to suffering. The trip reaffirmed his belief, "that to remain silent and indifferent is the greatest sin of all."

More recently, Wiesel was sent by the French President Francois Mitterand to Russia during a coup. He met with Mikhail Gorbachev immediately after his return to Moscow and, later, with both Gorbachev and Boris Yeltsin. He said that Gorbachev seemed very alone. It was the first time the two men had such a private meeting.

Wiesel credits Gorbachev with greatly changing the situation in Russia for the Jews.

THE U.S. HOLOCAUST MEMORIAL COUNCIL

In 1978, President Jimmy Carter appointed a Presidential Commission on the Holocaust. The 34-member Commission was headed by Wiesel. In 1979, the Commission visited Europe. At Treblinka, Wiesel described the setting "as bare as Stonehenge . . . where the names of those killed are not listed but the names of the cities are listed." They continued on to the Warsaw Ghetto, Auschwitz, Birkenau, and Babi Yar. At the various concentration camps, Commission members memorialized the dead.

Wiesel met with both Soviet and Polish officials. He wanted to obtain various records pertaining to their Jewish communities before and after the war. The records would help track histories of these communities. He also proposed to Soviet authorities a reference on a memorial in Kiev to the Jews killed at Babi Yar. Still, there is no public mention in Kiev of the 100,000 Jews who were murdered there.

In 1980, the Commission was renamed the U.S. Holocaust Memorial Council. The two mandates of the Council were to oversee the creation of a museum of the Holocaust (opened in April 1993) and to organize a *Yom Hashoah* ceremony for the Jewish holiday commemorating those who perished in the Holocaust. Wiesel chaired the Council until 1986.

THE CONGRESSIONAL GOLD MEDAL OF ACHIEVEMENT

On April 19, 1985, President Ronald Reagan presented the Congressional Gold Medal of Achievement to Wiesel at a ceremony in the White House. The medal recognized Wiesel's contributions as chairman of the U.S. Holocaust Memorial Council, as a man advancing the cause of human rights and as a literary scholar. Reagan's scheduled visit to West Germany clouded the ceremony with controversy.

Reagan planned to visit Bitburg, West Germany, to place a wreath at a cemetery where German soldiers and members of the SS, the elite guard, are buried. For Reagan, it would be part of a reconciliation trip to West Germany. Reagan's visit inflamed both Jewish and veterans' groups. The President publicly stated that he "did not want to visit the [Dachau] camp, in order not to reawaken memories" and "that most German soldiers in the cemetery were as much victims of the Nazis as were the Jewish inmates of the camps."

Once Reagan presented the medal to Wiesel, he immediately gave it to his son. Then Wiesel addressed his sadness and distress over Reagan's decision in the following words: "That place [Bitburg], Mr. President, is not your place. Your place is with the victims of the SS. . . . For I have seen the SS at work, and I have seen their victims. They were my friends. They were my parents."

In accepting the medal, Wiesel said, "It was given to me by the American people for my writing, teaching and for my testimony. . . . I have learned that the Holocaust was a unique and uniquely Jewish event, albeit with universal implications. . . . I have learned the danger of indifference, the crime of indifference. . . . But I have also learned that suffering confers no privileges . . . and I believe, we believe, that memory is the answer, perhaps the only answer."

A few hours later, after the ceremony, Reagan approached Wiesel in private. He asked Wiesel to accompany him on the trip to Bitburg. Wiesel was stunned by this invitation and immediately rejected it. On May 5, 1985, Ronald Reagan placed the wreath at Bitburg.

Wiesel saw the Reagans a year after Bitburg. Wiesel was one of eleven foreign-born, naturalized U.S. citizens to be presented by Reagan with a statue at the 1986 Liberty Weekend. Wiesel said he felt bad for Reagan and that with "Nancy there, it was no good. She was so possessive of Reagan." He thought it was a very uncomfortable moment for Reagan.

THE NOBEL PEACE PRIZE

In 1986, Wiesel humbly accepted the Nobel Peace Prize for speaking out about various humanitarian causes. At the ceremony, on December 10, in Oslo, Wiesel took the podium, accompanied by his son.

In his speech, Wiesel reaffirmed his humanitarian beliefs: "Sometimes we must interfere. When human lives are endangered, when human dignity is in jeopardy, national borders and sensitivities become irrelevant. Wherever men or women are persecuted because of their race, religion or political views, that place must — at that moment — become the center of the universe."

The "universal" Wiesel cannot stop speaking out against atrocities. "Why not let the unbearable recede? Simply because we can't. Last time, it was the killing of Jews — then the attempt to annihilate humanity itself — between the two came the sin of indifference. For, if we forget, next time indifference will no longer be a sin — it will be a judgment."

He has spoken out about atrocities in South Africa, Argentina, Cambodia, Biafra, Ethiopia and about the maltreatment of the Vietnamese "boat people." He has been an eyewitness to their pain and has spoken up from their silence. After the My Lai massacre in Vietnam, Wiesel was involved with a group that chartered a plane to get there and help. More recently, he visited the Miskito Indians of Nicaragua to obtain firsthand reports of their suffering under the Sandinista regime.

He has been asked about reconciling his views with the suffering and pain of the Palestinians. Wiesel's response has been that, as a Jew, his sympathies are for the Jewish state first and foremost. He has seen the Jews when they were weak, and he can't go against the state of Israel. He does see improvements in the Mideast with the possibility of a peace conference. With regard to the Palestinians, he has said he does feel for their anguish and pain yet deplores anything that leads to violence.

In 1990, Wiesel conducted an informal dialogue with John Cardinal O'Connor, which later became a book titled *A Journey of Faith*. They discussed anti-Semitism, apartheid, world peace and nuclear arms.

In that same year, Wiesel published *Evil and Exile* with Philippe de Saint-Cheron (an archivist with the Museum of France), a book much less personal than *Conversations with Elie Wiesel* by Harry James Cargas (updated in 1992), which deals with such topics as the controversy over Kurt Waldheim's treatment of Jews during World War II, death as injustice, the value of repentance, and suffering. It was also in 1990 that another of Wiesel's books appeared, *From the Kingdom of Night*, in which the text of his remarks to President Reagan about Bitburg are printed as Wiesel's testimony in a French court on Klaus Barbie, the infamous Butcher of Lyons. These are personal reminiscences with literary, philosophical, theological and political reflections as well.

Through his establishment of the Elie Wiesel Foundation for Humanity, Wiesel has not only promoted specifically educational projects such as national essay contests for college students dealing with human rights topics but has also initiated several worldwide gatherings of world figures to discuss international problems. One conference, in Paris in 1988, brought together Nobel Prize winners to discuss ways they could act in concert to ease world tensions; another was titled "The Anatomy of Hate" and took place in Oslo in 1990. This latter conference, co-hosted by The Norwegian Nobel Committee, included such personages as President Vaclav Havel, President Francois Mitterand, Nelson Mandela, Nadine Gordimer, Günter Grass, John Kenneth Galbraith, Yelena Bonner and others. A follow-up gathering under the same title took place the following year in Moscow, co-hosted by *Ogonyok* magazine.

Wiesel continues to write newspaper and magazine commentaries on current affairs, lectures widely throughout the world (he has been awarded seventy-three honorary degrees from colleges and universities in the United States, Canada, France, Israel, Finland, and Argentina, among others), and is now working on his memoirs. He continues to visit the world's trouble spots to be of whatever service he can. Most recently he visited the former Yugoslavia, inspecting firsthand the war zones and prisoner-of-war camps in Bosnia.

THE WORDS OF ELIE WIESEL

Although dominated by Jewish themes, strong questions and provocative thematic debates make Wiesel's work widely accessible.

There are two main dilemmas in his work: the struggle to convey a message that is simply impossible to convey and to convince a public that this message is true. The Holocaust was a true event, yet the atrocities were too horrific to be believed.

Wiesel has written a few books on the Holocaust. Rather than make this work routine, he has left a lasting impression on his readers with the power of just a few pieces. Wiesel abhors the trivialization of the Holocaust. He feels that art and Auschwitz, theatre and Auschwitz, are totally incompatible. There is no place for either art or theatre in Auschwitz or vice versa.

He has said he is writing something on the number of Holocaust writers who have committed suicide. There have been a few Holocaust writers to do so since the war: Josef Wulf, Paul Celan, Tadeusz Borowski, and, most recently, Jerzy Kosinski, whose first book was reviewed by Wiesel in *The New York Times*. Wiesel was greatly saddened by his death. He has also mentioned the loss of his friend Paul Celan, who killed himself by drowning in the Seine River in Paris. As he understands, it wasn't the loss of memory that pushed these authors to suicide; it was that language failed them. Words fail these men in their mission to communicate. The fear that words will fail him is also a great fear of Wiesel's.

NIGHT

One eloquent passage in *Night* describes what changed Wiesel's life forever:

> Never shall I forget that night, the first night in camp, which has turned my life into one long night, seven times cursed and seven times sealed. Never shall I forget that smoke. Never shall I forget the little faces of the children, whose bodies I saw turned into wreaths of smoke beneath a silent blue sky.
>
> Never shall I forget those flames which consumed my faith forever.
>
> Never shall I forget that nocturnal silence which deprived me, for all eternity, of the desire to live. Never shall I forget these moments which murdered my God and my soul and turned my dreams to dust. Never shall I forget these things, even if I am condemned to live as long as God Himself. Never.

Night was originally written as an 800-plus-page memoir in Yiddish. Now, it's condensed to 109 pages. In writing *Night*, Wiesel broke a ten-year, self-imposed vow of silence. The vow represented his firm belief that the Holocaust was an event too sacred to waste words on, too earth-shattering to be trivialized.

Francois Mauriac, the Nobel laureate whom Wiesel had previously interviewed, took the manuscript to the publisher and provided the introduction for the book. *Night* is dedicated to Wiesel's parents and his sister Tzipora, who perished at Auschwitz.

Early in the book, Wiesel describes the deportation of all foreigners from Sighet (as opposed to the later deportations of the Jews only) and the survival of one man, Moché the Beadle. Moché escapes from the Germans and returns to Sighet to tell of the horrors. He tells how the Gestapo killed the foreigners one by one. No one in Sighet believes his story. They mutter, "What an imagination."

What Wiesel saw with Moché is what he possibly feared with his writings: "*What an imagination.*" How is it possible that such terrible events occurred, events too horrific to be true? Moché came to Elie to tell his story and to warn the Jews what the Germans would do. This warning is consistent with the one Wiesel fills his humanitarian work with: these stories are true no matter how absurd they seem, and these words must reach the public.

Night is a story with no extras, told as austerely as possible — the tale is chilling and clear. Wiesel proclaims here and in his other work, "Having survived by chance, I was duty-bound to give meaning to my survival."

DAWN

Dawn, his second book, is dedicated to Francois Mauriac. Elisha, the main character, must deal with his awful transformation from a concentration camp survivor to an executioner of an innocent man. Elisha struggles with breaking the sixth Commandment (not to commit murder) and realizes that in doing so, he takes on the role of God. If man could become God, he would change the course of history.

Elisha is a member of the underground in Palestine fighting the ruling British. His past parallels Wiesel's. As a former Sorbonne student, he sat in a philosophy class trying to understand being the victim of genocide. Elisha wondered where God was during the war, what the meaning of suffering and surviving was, and about man's character and instincts.

His commander in the underground encourages Elisha to accept the idea that man is inhumane. By doing so, Elisha will be able to kill, and by killing the enemy, Elisha will rise again to his place as a Jew in history.

The story takes place during the night before Elisha is scheduled to kill John Dawson, an innocent Englishman. Dawson is revenge for the Jewish underground. At dawn, David Ben Moshe, a member of the underground, who was captured during an act of sabotage against the British, will be hanged.

Elisha's family of dead visits him during the night. The ghosts tell him, "We're present wherever you go, we are what you do." Elisha argues with his dead grandmother that he was born an idealist, not an executioner. For Elisha to kill just once means that he will be a killer forever.

THE ACCIDENT

The Accident, Wiesel's third book, is dedicated to Dr. Paul Braunstein. Braunstein saved Wiesel after his accident in Times Square. Again, there are numerous similarities between the narrator, Eliezer, and Wiesel.

The narrator gets hit by a cab in Times Square and spends a long period in the hospital. He is near death when he enters the hospital and fights the doctor. Eliezer sides spiritually and mentally with death until he chooses to live again.

Eliezer has survived a concentration camp and reminisces about a suicide attempt when he wanted to jump overboard as he journeyed across the ocean to America. Wiesel, too, thought of suicide by jumping overboard, but his commitment to write brought him back to life.

The Accident contains a passage about adulation for having survived, and Wiesel's feelings have not wavered regarding this. Eliezer is told, "Someone thinks you are a saint" because "you've suffered a lot . . . only saints suffer a lot." Eliezer responds, "What a joke. Saints are dead . . . but me, look at me, I'm alive." With his suffering, Wiesel does not want the respect of those who haven't suffered or the canonization that belongs to the saints; he merely wants peace and simple understanding that survival carries a weight and a responsibility of its own.

Another strong theme in *The Accident* is suffering. Eliezer and his girlfriend, Kathleen, represent opposites. Eliezer has been thrown into the suffering and wages a war between life and death. He chooses life. Kathleen's life has no suffering. She chooses to be consumed by suffering and chooses death.

GOD AND THE HOLOCAUST

Wiesel's work speaks of spiritual matters without alienating his secular audience. He provocatively discusses God and the presence or absence of God during the war in his works. God appears and disappears in *Night* and in most of his Holocaust literature.

Once in the camps, Wiesel was invited by a Rosh yeshiva (head of a yeshiva — a place for young men to study the Bible) and his two colleagues to a trial of God. The tribunal proclaimed that God was wrong and guilty for the genocide, not man. How could God have allowed the Holocaust to happen?

As a young man, Wiesel could understand man's inhumanity. He could read the history of the Jews to see that persecution has always existed. But God's inaction/action during the war? For this there was no clear answer.

Ask Wiesel if he believes that God existed during the Holocaust, and he'll tell you that the Holocaust could not have happened with a God and could not have happened without a God. But how could such a God allow his chosen people to be so terribly persecuted and not have stopped it? Wiesel will say that the covenant between God and his chosen people was broken during the Holocaust but that God always exists. He says you have to believe in God to be angry with him.

Marginal Thoughts on Yiddish

by ELIE WIESEL

There are certain songs that I can sing only in Yiddish. There are certain prayers that only Jewish grandmothers whispered in a twilight mood. There are jokes that ring true only in Yiddish. There are little stories whose magic and secret can be transmitted only by the Yiddish language, so permeated with sorrow and longing. There are times that race like the hands of clocks gone mad, from the source to an invisible abyss where *Yiddishkeit*, which encompasses Yiddish, is the only safety. There is a love that binds me to Yiddish and to all things that Yiddish once incorporated or at least reflected. So I feel compelled to speak about precisely this love.

To clarify? To explain? Love stands higher than reason. Would it occur to anyone to ask me why I have dark eyes? I love Yiddish because I was born with Yiddish. My first words were spoken in Yiddish. My first thoughts were formulated in Yiddish. I translated my first prayers into Yiddish.

For me Yiddish is my childhood years. Yiddish is a kingdom all its own. Everything can be found in Yiddish: charm and a knowing smile, goodness and envy, greatness and pettiness, knowledge and ignorance.

Words are like people, after all: rich and poor, tall and short, royal and inflated, old and bent, as well as young and newly formed. For example, take a sentence, analyze it, immerse yourself in it, and you will uncover generations of Jews who come from all corners of the Diaspora. True, the same can be said of other languages. But show me a people that has borne so much eternity through so many lands.

I read and heard Yiddish not only at home. I have found it in outlandish places. Listen to a story.

In the late fifties, together with two Israeli friends, I made a

Written in 1967, this essay originally appeared in the *Jewish Daily Forward* and was translated from the Yiddish by Irving Abrahamson. It is printed by permission of the author.

coast-to-coast journey by car through America. Somewhere in Arizona we suddenly saw a signboard that aroused our childish fantasy: "If you want to see Indians, come to their tent." "Indians?" we shouted. "Of course we very much want to see Indians. We have never seen Indians except in the movies." What did it matter if the side road took over one and a half hours? What will a Jew not do to have an encounter with Indians?

At last we reached the tent. A red-skinned Indian, dressed in the manner of his tribe, wearing a feathered headdress and with a huge pipe in his hand, greeted us politely. "Perhaps you would like to buy something from us?" My friends bought some presents. "Where do you come from?" he wanted to know. "From Paris by way of New York," I answered. My friends, on the other hand, said, "From far away." It was senseless to say they came from Israel. Why should an Indian know of a Jewish state? "If so," said the Indian, "you are welcome guests. Perhaps you would write something in my guest book." "With pleasure," we all answered. How can one deny an Indian anything? In order to give our visit a special character, I wrote my name in Hebrew. "What?" the Indian shouted in Yiddish, his face aflame. "You are Jews?" It turned out the "Indian" was really a Galitzianer Jew, a member of the saving remnant, who had found out that it is good business to be an Indian in Arizona.

What I found out is that America is indeed a golden land, that even the Indians speak Yiddish here.

Moreover, who does not speak Yiddish here? So many words have broken through into daily American speech it can almost seem that until we came here, the Americans must have been silent. Furthermore, today they love Yiddish. What comedian doesn't throw a few Yiddish expressions into his monologues? Who does not know that Sholem Aleichem — or, as they call him, Mr. Aleichem — is a genial humorist? There is a Jewish actor who has now really conquered Broadway with his Jewish jokes. He speaks half Yiddish and half English, and the whole world laughs. So our Sholem Aleichem is right, after all. Laughter is healthy. Broadway tells us to laugh.

This means Yiddish is good for laughter or for tears. One must look to other languages for neutral situations. For us, situations are either very good or very bitter. Though the Rambam has counselled us always to take the middle way, the King's Road, it is not so simple to heed him. When the sun shines, all creation is radiant. When it is dark, the darkness is as thick as in the grave. Since the destruction of the Temple, Jews have invariably lived in extreme circumstances. No one carries such a burden of sorrow, and no one conquers the sorrow with such stubbornness and such joy. The Vilna Gaon used to say that "You shall enjoy yourself in your festivals" is the most difficult commandment in the Torah. It is often difficult to rejoice, but the Torah commands it, so one rejoices as one is supposed to, with all one's might and with all one's soul. In spite of the fact that we cannot sing, we sing with all our strength. In spite of the fact that we cannot feel the taste of happiness, we must proclaim the right of the Jew to be happy. In spite of the fact that our enemies want us to live in terror, we conquer terror, and we shout joyously that it is good to be a Jew after all. Often I fail to understand how, in the profoundest depths of Auschwitz nights, experienced, wise, sensitive Jews were able to sing Sabbath melodies while death lurked in every hole, while flames coiled up to the heavenly temples. Where did they take the imagination and the strength to say, "They shall rejoice from Your goodness," *there* where the enemy had destroyed the last bit of good and the last bit of joy?

No other language in the world is capable of portraying those times of night. Without Yiddish, Holocaust literature would be without a soul. I know there are those who write in other languages. But there is no comparison. The most authentic works about the Holocaust, whether in prose or in poetry, are in Yiddish.

Is it because Yiddish has a past, a tradition of lamenting Jewish misfortune, or is it because most of the martyrs grew up in a Yiddish environment? Let the specialists solve the mystery.

I know only one thing: if not for my first book, which I wrote in Yiddish, if not for my Yiddish memories, all my other books would have remained silent.

CAN WE BRING THE MESSIAH?:
AN INTERVIEW WITH ELIE WIESEL

by HARRY JAMES CARGAS

HJC: Here we are some forty years after the end of World War II. Have we learned anything from the great tragedy, particularly from the Holocaust?

EW: In order to learn you have to deal with knowledge. I am not sure that the knowledge that we have of that Event brings us closer to the Event. It's a very strange Event because the knowledge of it removes us from it instead of the opposite. Usually knowledge brings us closer to people, to ideas. Not in this case. The more I read about it the less I understand it. And yet, no other tragedy or no other event has been as documented as this one has. From both sides everybody has written: the victims belatedly and the perpetrators themselves; the onlookers. The only one who has not spoken is probably God. And yet, in spite of the hundreds and hundreds of documents and books that are available to us, the knowledge is limited. We still don't know what really went on when the encounter took place between the killer and his victim. We don't know really what went on during the last minute when the parents and their children left one another. We don't really know what happened that made some go silently and others with prayers and others still with weapons in their hands. This is of course a different kind of knowledge, but this is the only knowledge that matters. The truth and that knowledge have not been given yet.

HJC: A kind of moral knowledge as opposed to historical knowledge?

EW: A philosophical knowledge, a metaphysical knowledge. In this respect the historians are performing a very important duty

This interview originally appeared in *Holocaust and Genocide Studies*, Volume I, 1986, pp. 5-10. It is reprinted by permission of the author.

and they fulfill it beautifully. I think they have done more than the others in the field of relating the Event to our generation and to others. But they are not a great help. In a strange way, any survivor has more to say than all the historians combined about what happened.

HJC: How do you relate what happened then to the world situation today?

EW: Well, I learned now what I learned forty years ago. It is a lesson in humility. To me it teaches humility first of all. If we recognize our limitations, whatever we do is limited. If we don't recognize that then we are in error. As for today, I think that the catastrophes that befell our generation since the war (we speak of one generation as forty years; in Biblical terms forty years marked one generation), this generation that suffered so many catastrophes, I am convinced that all of them somehow are related to that Event. All of them. The cynical attitude of the world with Cambodia, and Pol Pot, and the Khmer Rouge trying to kill the other half of his people and then to accept it, famine in Ethiopia and in Africa where, of all things, six million people are threatened by death because of hunger — whatever we throw out every day in America alone could be enough to save hundreds of thousands of children in Ethiopia — this indifference to other people's suffering is directly related to the indifference of the world that prevailed among mankind then. Above all, the nuclear menace that hangs upon us, the indifference of mankind toward the nuclear menace, is directly related to the indifference of the world to the Jewish tragedy then, with one exception. We have learned something: that the condition today is no longer a sin, it's a punishment. If we let it happen, I think we will become victims of our own indifference.

HJC: There is a distinction made by some sociologists about the way we look at ourselves or the way we lead our lives. They distinguish the "me" from the "beyond me." We seem to have very little sense of "beyond me," of responsibility to future generations.

EW: And yet no generation has had so many needs available to it or the capability of knowing what is happening in other places. Imagine, we can see live broadcasts from Ethiopia. We can see live broadcasts from Cambodia. While the Vietnam War was going on, the war was brought to us in our dining rooms. And lo and behold, people could eat while they were seeing what was happening. People were dying while people were eating. Whose fault is it? I think it's true that we have not managed to communicate the lessons or the images, or the lack of images and tones, the undertones, of that tragedy. I believe that the main objective, the main goal, of telling the story is to sensitize people. And if people are still insensitive, that means we have failed.

HJC: But historically doesn't it seem that we are sensitized, yet only for a short while, and then we become indifferent again, whether the tragedy is the prison riot in Attica, the hunger in Ethiopia, the slaughters in Central America?

EW: True. But still I believe that this tragedy that we speak about was so different. It was unique. It must have produced and provoked a unique response, a unique sensitizing effect. Because it was unique, it would last; but it doesn't. However, there are some people, some young people, who are changed by it. Therefore, that is the redeeming value of our work. Here and there you will find one student, one leader, or one person who enters that literature, that body of literature, and emerges a changed person. That person is changed for life.

HJC: So is the world being kept in existence because of the "ten just people" who are so moved?

EW: Absolutely. If not, I don't think we would be able to do what we are doing, you and I, and those of us who do it. It's because of the minority; there are very few who listen and who are ready to listen, which means to accept an incommensurate amount of suffering.

HJC: Is the indifference more prominent in some areas than others, or is this a generational, worldwide phenomenon in your opinion?

EW: It is worldwide, but it is "towards whom." That means somehow society today has a selective sensitivity. Some people are sensitive only to one category of victims and not to the others. That is wrong. I believe that what we are teaching is sensitivity, period. If one is sensitive to one injustice, one must be sensitive to all injustice, which will never be at the expense of others. For two thousand years the Jewish tragedy was singled out as one that people could not pay attention to. For two thousand years there were great humanists who were humanists and at the same time remained anti-Semitic. Knowing but not knowing what they were doing or saying or writing. To me it was one of the great shocks of my adult life when I discovered that people who used to be my heroes — Voltaire, Kant — were anti-Semites. It was possible then to be treated as human, to even aspire to elevate themselves, to portray themselves as humanists, and at the same time to hate Jews. A child said, "When I suffer don't I cry, don't I bleed?" What does it mean? It means "Why aren't you sensitive to my pain?" People were not sensitive to our pain. The culmination of all that was, of course, Auschwitz. I wonder often whether Western society would have remained as passive had the six million victims not been all Jewish; such numbers and such measures, total extermination. I wonder. Today it is more politicized. When Israel suffers, people remain insensitive to its suffering. I believe that sensitivity must be broadened and deepened, and to be sensitive to Jewish suffering means we are sensitive to all suffering: Central America, Central Asia, Africa, or the dissidents in Russia.

HJC: How do I become more sensitive? How, when I know, do I help others to become more sensitive?

EW: First, as Malraux says, "What is literature?" It is an act of transforming experience into consciousness. You can do that by reading, by working and, in your case, especially by writing. You know how to use words. How? By taking a position and speaking out. I know in my own humble way, my restricted way, whenever I became aware of an injustice, I tried to learn, first of all, as much as I could about it. Speak about it, write about it. I was in South Africa, I wrote about the Sowetos. I wrote of my shame as a white person. I never felt ashamed as a white person except when I was there. The outrage one feels. Biafra. Miskito Indians. It's the Jew in me that felt the outrage. It's the Christian in you that should feel that outrage. Or the writer in you, or the teacher in you, the essayist, the moralist in you. If you do that then those who read you will do the same, hopefully.

HJC: Then there is, in a sense, the opposite teacher. I'm thinking of the media particularly now. How they contribute to an atmosphere of indifference. Even Holocaust jokes, some told by Jewish comedians. The general atmosphere of acquisitiveness and "me now" that makes us indifferent to the problems of others. Suffering is not the pretty life.

EW: The media has not fulfilled, at least until now, its duty in this respect. But then we cannot be too critical because it is a very special genre, as you know. The media can be the best and can be the worst. And usually they try to combine, they try to compromise. They cannot write only about one subject. They must write about all the subjects. I have not written compromises when it comes to certain issues or to certain concerns. That is my luxury. I can write a book only with one subject. A newspaper cannot do that. I think *Life* magazine did it once. They devoted a whole issue to Hiroshima. I think John Hersey wrote it. It's a great moment in history.

HJC: But it hasn't been followed up much.

EW: Not too much.

HJC: Documentaries perhaps on television.

EW: Yes.

HJC: How do you see us, as a society, approaching these problems? Is it through Amnesty International, through the United Nations? How?

EW: I have the feeling that in this respect the impetus came from the base, from the grass roots. It is because of some people who began teaching in some classes and some students who became teachers then that later on an awareness was created. In other words, it is not, let's say in a case which is so close to us, it's nothing like the United States Holocaust Memorial Council created the awareness; it's the awareness that created the United States Holocaust Memorial Council. Because of that, we increase the awareness and, as a result, you have now all the other cities that try to follow our example, and we have so many city centers for Holocaust studies, and the more the better. I am all for that. But it is the simple human gesture, the simple human response on the part of an individual here and an individual there, that the mood was changed in the country. Now, once it is done, organizations should step in. Amnesty International is important, and the Council I think is doing important educational work. Governments should adopt laws. I, for instance (but I'm not a lawyer), would like to see some legal steps taken against those who deny that the death camps existed. But of course I know the problems: the First Amendment, the freedom of expression. But I would like to see that. After all, what they say is that I am a liar and that all those who wrote books about their experiences, all the survivors, are liars. There must be some way of protecting this small minority, the most tragic of all, the minority of the survivors. It doesn't exist.

HJC: I remember at the Liberators Conference we held in Washington when a British jurist suggested that a law should be passed in all lands to make it a crime to say that the Holocaust never happened. He received an ovation for that remark.

EW: I'm for it.

HJC: Now I would like to talk about your role personally. You have been involved, among so much else, in Cambodia. You have gone there and to South Africa, as you mentioned, and Central America. You have worked on behalf of the people who have rights problems in Argentina and Paraguay, Ethiopia now. You have had some effect on Arab-Jewish relations. You have Arab readers and admirers. How do you keep on going?

EW: It's more and more difficult, but what else could I do? For me it's easy. There is nothing else that I know how to do. I often think that if I could not be a teacher and a writer I would probably be the unhappiest person in the world. I wouldn't know how to sustain my family. I don't know anything else. At the same time, after all, I feel that all of us who survived, we survived by accident. We didn't do anything to survive; it was sheer accident. Somebody else could be here in my place and speak to you and probably say the same things. So I am responsible not only for myself but for that person who could be here and speak to you in my place. Every moment, therefore, is a moment of grace, and I must justify it. That doesn't mean that I think about it twenty-four hours a day, not at all. I lead a normal life. I love my students and, of course, above all, my family, my son. I study the Talmud. And when I study the Talmud every day, I don't think about atrocities. And when I write about the Bible or the prophets or the Talmud or Hassidic masters I don't think about it. We need everything. Of course there is knowledge that I must justify every moment of my existence.

Once you have that conviction, it's easy. If not, I would be punished myself. If I wouldn't have gone to Cambodia I would have felt badly. So that the fatigue on one hand is opposed to feeling badly for years on the other. So the fatigue doesn't mean a thing. If I wouldn't go now to Ethiopia it would be the same thing. I would feel badly. So it's easier to go than not to go.

HJC: You said in our book, "One must be obsessed today." This is the kind of obsession you have.

EW: Call it passion, fervor, obsession. But we all are obsessed. That is the special impact that this world — the world of Auschwitz — has on us and all of us who lived it through or those who deal with it as scholars, as writers, as commentators. Once you enter it you are obsessed; you are no longer the same person. You are inhabited by its fire.

HJC: How did you enter it?

EW: I was brought into it. I didn't choose to enter it. I wrote about it in *Night*. I was a young boy, and one night I discovered I was no longer at home, that I was in exile. I discovered that everybody else was in exile. Every word I would ever utter would be in exile. Every gesture I would ever make would be in exile. Every prayer I would ever formulate would be in exile. So that was how I entered it.

HJC: Others were brought in also who survived and seem not to be so actively involved.

EW: I think they had their reasons. They felt it wouldn't be understood. And those who would understand wouldn't know. The temptation of silence is very strong. It still is. Not to speak about it, because nobody would understand.

HJC: Does this, in your judgment, sometimes culminate in suicide for some of them?

EW: Yes. I want to understand it, and it's easy to understand. So many writers committed suicide. And I understand why. It's the total despair that you spoke and nobody listened. Therefore it is easier not to speak. Because then you think maybe, if I spoke, . . . maybe if I had spoken, things would be different. One of my closest friends, Piotr Rawicz, committed suicide. His book, *Blood from the Sky*, is a masterwork. Take even Romain Gary, although he left other explanations for his suicide. But in truth he also tackled the problem. There was an old woman, Rivka Guber. She also committed suicide. I'm sure that she committed suicide because at one point she wrote a book about it. And I treasure that book. She interviewed survivors from my region in Transylvania. You don't enter that world with impunity.

HJC: What is the relationship between writing and justice?

EW: It's a sense and feeling of total impotence, that there can never be justice. I believe that writing is a way of correcting injustices. It's an attempt to say that we do justice; and unfortunately we have only a hope — it cannot be attained. The only justice would be if I could bring back, if not six million, at least one person to life. But I cannot. The only other justice I would accept would be — and I mean it very profoundly — very sincerely, the coming of the Messiah.

HJC: Writing can assist and contribute to this?

EW: No. I wish I could believe that, but I don't think so. Only the other justice. That means there are two folds of justice that I would accept. One, if my writing could bring back to life, not only to the imaginary life but to real life, at least one person, one child. But I cannot. Or on a larger scale, on a more theological scale, that's why I don't feel any theology of the Holocaust is possible except this one: if the Messiah were to come.

HJC: I want to wind up by going back to something that you said earlier. The victims have spoken, the perpetrators have spoken, the indifferent have spoken. God has not spoken. Is the only way, then, for God to speak with the coming?

EW: The only way. The only way: the coming of the Messiah. This is the only response possible because, otherwise, nothing is a response. But here you know that Israel is said to be a response. This places on Israel such a terrible burden. There is no response. Maybe Hiroshima was a response. As always, whatever happens happens to Jews first and then to others. If you don't heed that answer, be careful. We are not heeding that answer. That has been the source of my anguish. The knowledge that we have of that Event is so poor, and, therefore, the lesson so limited. It is maybe the wrong lesson.

HJC: And yet "the silence of God is God."[1]

EW: That's not an answer, it's only a question. Of course, whenever we deal with God, it's always a question.

NOTES

1. Elie Wiesel, *Ani Maamin* (New York: Random House, 1973) 87.

Twelve Poems of the Holocaust

by LOUIS DANIEL BRODSKY

*For Elie Wiesel, whose defiance of Silence
has made survivors of us all.*

Third-Reich Birds

The birds keep an uneasy peace with people —
Even predacious jays
And chicken hawks scanning the sides of highways
For signs of carrion or quick flesh.
Only the crows, their jet-stained contemptuousness
Too ingrained to render them timorous,
Don't flinch at the twitch of a human eye,
Shift of a twig, or leaf-seizure.

Something in their arrogant reflexes,
Numinously or naturally inspired,
Necessarily controls their spectral strategies
To dominate the space they occupy.
Whenever I see one or a *Korps,*
Nearby or at a distance,
My whole body convulses with cold fear;
They have a horrible reputation for breaking treaties.

Cracow, Now!

Defeated, exiled, indefensibly committed,
Those dispensable souls
Relegated to the ghetto in Cracow!
Bankers, Talmudic scholars, grocers, musicians,
Strict, disciplined family men
Whose reverential Leahs, Rachels, Miriams
Bore in pride brilliant children!
Ghosts now, still guiding wheelbarrows
Filled with pillows and sheets
From cultured salons in family estates
To ventilator shafts, attics,
And dead airspace between rooms
In hovels cluttering Memory's tear ducts.

The metamorphosis of three centuries
Accomplished in months: Jew-Lice-Typhus.
Then the Madagascar Plan.
In the end, only Hitler's witless tactics —
Matching his storm troopers
Against Russia's forces of winter —
Could suspend the Final Solution
For tribes confined to greenhouses
Producing a variety of Venus's-flytraps
So profuse neither Linnaeus
Nor Darwin could have classified them:
Auschwitz, Treblinka, Belzec,
Dachau, Bergen-Belsen, Birkenau!

Just writing their bleak syllables chokes me.
Each is a puff of black smoke
Escaping crematory stacks
Punctuating skylines of my verse,
Each a caesura too frequently breathed.
This morning, four decades downwind,
The measures of my sanity dwindle.
I, too, as messenger for the Dispossessed,
Wearing a "J" on my brain-band,
Push all my earthly belongings, paltry words,
In a rickety wheelbarrow across the years,
Toward precarious lodging
In the ghettos of *your* unsuspecting ears.

Himmler at Auschwitz, 1942

A dim image of Heinrich Himmler
Simmers on Imagination's back burner:
He stands at a safe distance
Just in front of Auschwitz's newly finished
Disinfection facility;

Standing at histrionic attention
In his spit-shined jackboots,
SS uniform, cap with patinous brim,
With engraved dress revolver decorating his hip
Like icing on a wedding cake;

Standing statuesquely
With an inscrutable expression,
Waiting for the first thousand victims
To emerge from the very first "Special *Aktion*,"
Waiting with the patience of Job;

Standing, as low moaning
Slowly metamorphoses into hysterical prayers
That sift through hastily nailed boards
And lift in a sick-sweet mixture
Of gasping, choking bellows and catalepsy gas;

Standing rigidly, gold-rimmed glasses
Focusing to a higher power his myopic eyes
On the montage of asphyxiated, naked humans
Being rolled away in coal cars,
Heaved into open pits along the track,

Covered with lime, and left festering
While less fortunate deportees
Sporting Star of David patches
Continue backtracking to load the rest,
Freshly sprayed with insecticide;

Standing in astonished admiration
Even after the last corpse has been dispatched,
As though his boots were glued to the earth,
No member of his staff
Daring to make the slightest move to disperse

Despite nausea each can almost hear
Gnawing his gurgling bowels,
Or willing to inform this man of vision,
This mastermind of the Third Reich,
Who promises to purge Germany

Of Jew-vermin, Gypsies, and sexual perverts,
That this initial supply has run dry,
The next freight-train load
Not scheduled to arrive
From the Russian front for two days yet;

Standing like Christ being shown
The glorious Kingdoms of the world
As if from God's throne;
Standing in dazed amazement, reverential,
Contemplating the colossal possibilities of his revelation.

Valediction Forbidding Despair,
   Cracow Ghetto, 1943

This summer is Treblinka;
Its regimental months are ovens that arrest us
In bloodless custody,
Dress us in evaporating memory-ashes.
Victims, like crickets
Scratching dryness from limbs,
Chant hymns through lips that shape the air
With unfinished kisses;
We listen with bleeding disbelief,
Knowing soon we'll meet in *Gan Eden*.

Musicians, carpenters, midwives, physicians,
Zionists and assimilationists
Yet amidst us
Guard the darker silences
Of those who crowd naked each day
In boxcars and chambers,
Where almond-perfumed night descends.
Premonitions race down chutes
To steaming graves
Time spreads with quicklime and fertilizer.

But the spirit exists outside ideologies,
Or it should, anyway;
The end obliterates nothing, really,
Except flesh
And the evanescent death wish
To rest just long enough
To catch one's breath
Before resuming the necessary trek
Toward Memory's ultimate destination,
Resurrection.

Twilight

Only when he sits on his front stoop
Witnessing twilight drip blood
Does a tenacious sense of disillusionment
Infiltrate his defenses,
Rifle his desk, ransack his files,
And infect his mind with a hacker's virus
He knows will eventually blight
The entire pattern of historical events
He's spent a lifetime re-collecting,
Sequentially ordering,
Trying to explain and morally justify;
It's then he settles into a forlorn stupor.

His tongue-tied eyes glaze
As stomach and throat collaborate
In regurgitating the past
All over day's face and clothes,
Leaving a reeking pool of greenish drool
At memory's feet in which he'll wallow all evening.
In dismal moments such as this,
He shivers like a stalked rabbit
Sensing a hunter has it in the focus
Of his thousand-power scope
And is about to nail it to a cross-hairs crucifix.
He quivers, as if back at Auschwitz,

Suspecting these malevolent visions —
Issue of Scylla and Charybdis —
Lurk in a vortex beneath the surface,
Course between late afternoon and night,
Where light and darkness
Disguise themselves as Life and Death,
Silence and Keening, Luck and Misfortune,
And play odd-man-out,
Each side hoping to survive the other's Fate.
Maybe what keeps reminding him he died
Are sunballs, like today's,
He recalls having first seen in '44,

Through a crack in a boxcar door,
As he rode the last transport leaving Sighet
For dislocations he'd call home
The rest of Destiny's trip.
He dies each time he sees from his porch
Dawn dripping blood
From night's great, gaping uterus
Or envisions a rusty, gushing sun at dusk
Spilling the shrill, stillborn fetuses
Of a million children of Zion,
Filling his nostrils with menstrual stench
From a womb-tomb at Earth's dead center.

Liberation from Buchenwald

He awakens at 5:00 a.m.
Although early, it's too late
For his obscure dreams
To alert consciousness to his metamorphosis;
They retreat into Sleep's forest
Like squirrels scurrying behind trees
As a ghostly shape approaches,
Rushes past, and escapes its own shadow.

He emerges from an oneiric furnace
Up whose stack he's volitionlessly floated
Like memory-ashes issuing from chimneys:
Arms with blue, tattooed numerals,
Twisted gruel spoons,
Striped uniforms, worn-out sandals.
Peering through two million pairs of glasses,
He focuses his diminished vision,

Inspects his warped face in a mirror
For ghetto-etched reflections.
Vaguely he recognizes the corpse gazing back
As that Specter he'd met on the road,
Who, begging directions to a mass grave,
Would detain him just enough
To throw him incorrectably out of step
The rest of his snowy march home.

Friday Night Out

He's grown so used to living alone,
Living at home,
He never seems to leave anymore
Except on Friday nights,
When he eats at a neighborhood café;
There he sits amidst phantoms
Escaping flickering candle tips
Whose brass sticks are brick chimney stacks
From which he imagines his parents and sister —
Wax-fattened wicks dripping, evaporating —
Lifting into ashen oblivion.

Whether returning early or late
From his one indulgence,
He slips under freshly pressed shrouds,
Pulls up around his neck
Three woolen blankets, summer and winter,
And counts, from one million down,
Fleeceless Picasso-sheep
Leaping off invisible cliffs
Into Auschwitz pits beside his bed
Before sleep inundates him
With *Zyklon B*-guilements.

For three decades,
He's never abandoned hope
That just one Friday night
He'll glimpse his deported wife, Leah,
Shimmering in a golden, glowing halo
On the front stoop of his dreams,
Greeting him home, again.

Grodsky the Cobbler

Near the Delmar Loop in St. Louis
(No one knows for sure
In which tenement he dwells),
There lives and dies daily
A Jewish cobbler of shoes,
Who bears just above his bony wrist
Greenish-blue Auschwitz numerals
Obscenely tattooed to his skin
Like an oozing cicatrix,
Shapes crazily misaligned
Like figures floating in alphabet soup.

By trade a shoe repairer,
Anachronous, obsolete,
He still waits — sometimes all day
Without one person in need of his services —
To ply his skills despite near blindness,
Enfeeblement; an octogenarian
Who has no business doing business,
He yet paces sidewalks and crosses streets
As if back in Bremerhaven
Instead of this contemporary American ghetto
Inhabited by blacks, college students, and the elderly,

Where thirty years earlier
The City's most esteemed "kikes" resided —
University professors, symphony musicians,
Bankers, merchants, attorneys, surgeons,
The cream of Midwestern Jewry,
Who, not to their collective face
But always behind their back, were reviled,
Their display windows cracked, cemeteries desecrated —
Spurned because of their learning,
Fenced off by their affluence,
And, finally, betrayed by their success.

Half a century later, lapsing from consciousness,
This ash of a man stoops over his bench,
Apron strings cinching his waist
To keep his pants from falling to his shoes;
Shoes he's repaired so many times
Their original German leather no longer exists,
Nor do their soles remember the shapes
Of the *Vaterland*'s cobbles that wore them smooth
As he fled, his possessions possessed;
Shoes he maintains nonetheless,
In case he needs to make another hasty escape.

The Thorough Earth

He moves ahead by fits,
Suffers amnesiac fugues and hallucinations
Every few days or weeks,
Stutters, halts, fidgets unpredictably
Like needles of an EKG machine
Whenever he hears sirens
Or sees police; they arrest his thoughts,
Hurl him back to that Nazi Hell
Before he'd fled Berlin for Argentina,
Then to St. Louis, Missouri, his Elba.

Although more than forty years
Have worn away the most horrific details
Of gargoyled paranoia
That surmounted and drained his spirit's temple
In those ghettoed seasons
After that latter-day Wagner
Perforated the world's eardrums
With his demoniac baton,
He still sees in his mirrored eyes
Fear's shattered stained-glass windows,

Still realizes that beneath the smooth facade
His low-profiled anonymity projects,
The old trepidation festers.
Today he appears inordinately upset.
Whether it's graffiti recently splattered
On Sleep's side streets and alleys,
Cops surrounding a shot President
Pervading his TV screen,
Or swastikas taped to his shop windows,
He can't say with certainty.

Maybe it's the dust of *Kristallnacht*
Or just the sheer weight of years
Crushing his skull to dull pain,
Exploding his brain, quashing his spirit.
Abruptly he collapses in front of his store;
Blood gushes from his nostrils.
His vested suit, pressed dress shirt
Serve as makeshift shrouds
During the hour's hiatus
Before strangers identify his corpse.

Another forty-five minutes elapse
As police, city coroner, and ambulance
Conclude their routine removal of evidence
Suggesting Death ever arrived and left.
Before going, they padlock the door,
Place cards vaguely resembling "J"s
In his darkened display windows,
And outline in yellow chalk
The Star of David shape of his crumpled body
On the sanitized sidewalk.

Now silence descends;
Twilight shadows efface from his store sign
All traces of *Estate Diamonds*,
Leaving intact only his last name's first half:
*Frei*mann.
Briefly relieved, the empty street sighs
While fastidious Earth,
Elated over having satisfied her belated claims
On an unapprehended enemy,
Renews her search for the unexterminated.

The Book Burner

"Wherever they burn books they will also, in the end, burn human beings."
— *Heinrich Heine*

Yesterday afternoon,
At loose ends and without suitable alternatives
To relax his all-too-diffuse mind,
He decided to spend a few idle hours
Browsing through antique shops and used-book stores
In downtown St. Louis.
Scanning the precisely categorized titles
Swelling the shelves
Of Wagner's World-Wide Editions,
He noticed a sign on a case
Labeled "WW II,"
"Inquire at desk for Nazi materials,"
And, as if grasping a croker sack of hissing cobras
He knew better than to open,
Approached the owner to make his request.

Like a hibernating bear
Waking from millennial slumber
Or a nightmare exploding to the surface
Of this cave-dwelling seller's psyche,
The ghost of Gustav Wagner
Rose from his overstuffed sofa behind the register,
Disappeared into an opaque corridor,
His sanctum sanctorum,
And lumbered to the counter with a packet of pamphlets,
Each printed in cryptic, black-and-red,
Gothic calligraphy,
Some in English, some in German,
All dated, on the verso of the title page
Or at the foot of the back cover,
1938.

One title arrested and exterminated his thoughts
As though state agents had caught them
Breaking into the Ministry of Propaganda,
Where the Gestapo kept its documents
On perverts, Gypsies, idiots,
Syphilitics, malcontents, homosexuals,
And Christ-killing race defilers:
What to Do About the Jewish Question.
Petrified, he flipped through its brittle pages,
Felt himself grow nauseated.
Frantically, one fist clutching the sinister booklet,
He ran from the store into the street
And, unconscious of his *Aktion*,
Heaved it into the sun's sputtering ash heap,
Not even stopping to watch it ignite.

A Barren Marriage

Two survivors of the Holocaust,
Jewess and Jew,
Beautiful to each other,
Blessed keepers of the imperishable faith
That humored Pharaoh and Hitler,
Share a heritage of enduring frailty,

Squeeze each other in a breathless embrace
Millennially deep. They believe
Their impassioned arteries and veins,
Sympathetically pulsating,
Draining and refilling ancient reservoirs,
Circulate the entire fated history of their race.

In naked view of the ascending moon,
They tongue Dead Sea fluids
To quench their cells' thirst for salt,
Renew her menstrual cycle halted in the camps;
Then, gently blending egg and sperm,
They pray they'll create a child

Who just might survive them
Into a future when Gentile and Jew,
Moslem, Buddhist, and Hindu
Will kiss each other's exotic lips
Without offending anyone's God;
And always they fall asleep hoping, hoping.

Bringing Klaus Barbie to Trial

How many times must we return
To the scene of our hearts' crimes, dear Lord,
Before learning that cruelty and greed
Are qualities inherent in human doing
And that we repeat our least civilized acts
Not in defense nor from fear for our immortal spirits
But out of a perverse fascination with violence
That transcends infliction of pain on enemies
And disillusionment with those we most adore?

What diabolical impulses exhort us
To explore our darkest desires
By forcing hopeless souls to chew cyanide,
Shoving cowering, naked people into showers, ovens,
Dismembering breasts, genitalia, vital organs
From those tattooed with the dispersed Tribes' curse
In the fiendish pursuit to produce a Master Aryan Race
Composed of fair-haired, blue-eyed Teutonics,
Not hooknosed Jewesses and Jews?

Even now, I feel the rails quivering near Dachau,
Though my own senses can only imagine
That clattering death rattle of cattle cars
Crammed with lambs being transported to the slaughter,
Only imagine tasting that acrid blue-black dust
Rising from Auschwitz's factory stacks,
And, although I've visited these Masadas
In a thousand imperishable nightmares and daydreams,
Only imagine their ghosts still roaming Poland.

Is there no end to the genocidal torment of it all?
Can't confession and expiation
Relieve the burden of having to relive it indeterminately
Every time Memory backs up like a flooded gutter
Spewing debris into alleys,
Clogging shortcuts between forgetting and survival?
Why does it persist,
That banshee anthem of damned insanity?
Can't we sentence it to Silence once and forever?

Proclaiming the Silence

by FRANKLIN H. LITTELL

Looking back over twenty-two years of friendship with Elie
Wiesel calls to mind many dramatic events. In the entropy of the
universe, things fall apart. Where Elie goes, things jump to life.

On the occasion of our first season of any duration together, the
First Annual Scholars' Conference on the Holocaust and the Church
Struggle in 1970, I saw how electric his presence can be. The very
considerable interfaith gathering that heard his exchange with
Richard Rubenstein, as well as the thousands who have subsequently
read about it and talked about it, were dramatically introduced to
Elie's intellectual riposte. As a writer, he is a master of paradox; as
a religious philosopher, he is a master of dialectic.

Richard had told again of his conversation with Probst Heinrich
Grueber of Berlin. He had spoken of the way in which Grueber —
a fine man who had helped save many Jews from the Nazis and
who is appropriately remembered as a righteous rescuer at Yad Vashem
in Jerusalem — had reaffirmed the traditional explanations about
God's presence and absence in history. As they spoke, the tanks of
the occupier rolled through the streets under Grueber's windows.
Grueber acknowledged their presence as a sign of God's judgment
upon the German people, his own people, a viewpoint for which he
had the necessary bona fides. And then Grueber made the traditional
— one might almost say "classical" — Christian mistake: he went
propositional; he slid into an abstract and unfeeling generalization.
Probst Grueber, the good Christian and rescuer, once started, could
not stop until he had inferred that it had been God's will to send
Adolf Hitler, the exterminator of Europe's Jews, into history. [1]

Presented with this traditional Jewish and Christian God active
in history, Rubenstein said that he opted rather for a Canaanite
god, a god of place. Rubenstein defied the mystery. He broke the
dialectic in his own way. Since then, Richard Rubenstein has
modified some aspects of his passionate rejection of tradition. But

Previously unpublished, this tribute is printed by permission of the author.

Rubenstein's passion about that initial confrontation with Probst Grueber could be sympathized with, even if his response lacked the tragic note. Christendom, with its harsh and triumphalist theological propositions, has been driving sensitive Jews and gentiles into verbal expressions of unbelief for centuries.

Elie answered Richard in a way both deeply personal and sympathetic and in a way that also restored the mystery and the paradox. His message, "Talking and Writing and Keeping Silent," is a succinct and sensitive answer to a questing friend and also a reweaving of a network of dialectical tension that holds the world of the Bible together. [2]

As I stated in remarks quoted by Harry James Cargas in his book *Responses to Elie Wiesel*, one of Elie's major contributions to Jewish religious philosophy and Christian theology has been to liberate his listeners and readers to the debate with God.[3] Instead of cutting the mystery short by fleeing into conventional propositions or contemporary abstractions, however pious some of them may sound, we are invited to join Abraham and Moché the shammes and Elie himself in cross-examining God.

This is a radical break from the conventionally religious posture. For centuries both Christians and Jews have been schooled in the virtue of unquestioning obedience to authority, of unquestioning obedience to an authoritarian god and to those who claim to wield authority in his name. We have a large library of devotional books extolling the merit of submission and a mountain of folk sayings: "Keep your head down"; "Don't make waves"; "Obey those set above you"; "The powers that be are ordained of God."

In the heat of the church struggle, some Christians experienced — and those who survived the battle against the idolatry of the *Fuehrerstaat* have reported their experience to us — the uselessness and impotence of that theological line to those who were involved with the perpetrators. And out of the ashes of Auschwitz, Jewish teachers have arisen to tell of the dreadful price that traditional stance exacted of the victims. It is not too much to say that both the Christian resisters and the Jews in Hitler's empire were trapped not only by the brutal power of the Nazis and their collaborators; they were also trapped by ancient teachings of submission that were broken reeds and cut the hands that leaned on them.

Perhaps one of the greatest dimensions of Christian/Jewish cooperation in the post-Holocaust era will be the building up of our yet small shelf of books on conscientious objection and resistance. When does a fully human person have the right, indeed the duty, to resist public policy? What is the difference between resistance to a criminal government, an illegitimate government, and a legitimate government when committing wrong acts? These are fundamental questions that cannot be burked by Jews and Christians who have heard with hearing ears the stories of the Holocaust.

We hear much of the need for a demolition and reconstruction of theology after Auschwitz. A substantive section of the reconstruction will be a politics worthy of liberated men and women. This major contribution to democratic government and human rights will owe much to the message which Elie has brought us, a "liberation theology," if you will, that begins with the debate with God.

This reconstruction must be approached "in fear and trembling," as the Scriptures say, lest we slide easily into a new set of rigidities. And here another of Elie Wiesel's basic teachings presses forward: respect for *silence*. In the face of the deepest mystery of life and death, thoughtless utterance and premature closure are but the babbling of fools.

Telling the Story is difficult enough, but it must be done and let to do its work in the consciousness of individuals and societies. One of the most powerful tellings is the annual remembering, recapitulating and reenactment of the loss of the six million: *Yom Hashoah*. But now, after "forty years in the wilderness," the survivors and liberators and rescuers — and spectators — are beginning to talk about the lessons of the Holocaust.

We enter holy and dangerous ground. Elie Wiesel is a man of parables. Let me relate a parable:

> Marcus Licinus Crassus Murcianus, Governor General of Syria under Vespasian, was a man of great scientific interests. During his tour of duty in the east, he heard many tales about the region: its temple, its fanatic, ungovernable population, its palace, its desert, their porous rocks, its remarkable lake in which nothing could sink. Of an investigatory bent, taking nothing for granted, he had men thrown into the lake with their hands tied behind their backs, to see if the reports about the Dead Sea were true.
>
> Do not misunderstand: we are not dealing here with

cruelty, but with the passion of the intellect.[4]

One is reminded of the discussion between Adrian Leverkuhn, the scientist, and Dr. Zeitblom in Thomas Mann's *Doctor Faustus*. The scientist was impelled by a passion more powerful than love: intellectual curiosity. [5]

What a terrible thing it would be if our own lords of the campus should render the Holocaust harmless to mind and spirit! And that is precisely the present danger now that the intellectuals are beginning to look at that from which they have for forty years turned away their eyes.

Twenty years ago even the textbooks in European civilization or modern European history totally ignored the Holocaust. Most of them still do. But where the scientific work is going on, there are already signs of dangerous domestication of the data: using familiar phrases and unreconstructed systems of thought, theologians are writing about theodicy, sociologists are writing about racial prejudice, psychologists are writing about mob psychology, political scientists are writing about dictatorship, Marxist historians are writing about the revolt of the lower middle class . . . and all this in the name of the Holocaust!

Was the Holocaust really a result of irrational forces, of the unrestrained and unpredictable explosion of human emotions? It is a common mistake to think that the destruction of 60% of European Jewry and 33% of the Jews then in the world was primarily a result of sadism, cruelty, bestiality, bigotry. Those emotions are emphasized in the journals and autobiographies because, after all, these are human qualities we can portray and interpret. But blaming irrational emotions is much too easy, like making Hitler responsible for the whole thing.

Let me remind you of the role of Christendom and the failure of the church leaders. That confrontation is progressing, with its awesome implications for church teaching, preaching and acting. Let me mention a stonier ground just being opened up: the nature of the modern university. The Holocaust was planned, supervised and rationalized by professors and Ph.D.s — not to forget the M.D.s. The disposal of "life unworthy of life" (*Lebensunwertes Leben*), like the *Lebensborn* breeding program, was also a product of "the passion of the intellect."

Of all the wrongs inflicted on the victims, none after the fact would be worse than to approach the Holocaust in the same frame of mind as that displayed by the bureau chiefs who gathered with Heydrich at Wannsee in January of 1942 to approach the subject with the *Eiskalt* (ice cold) indifference to *Mentschlichkeit* (humanness) that Himmler considered proof of his officers' devotion to science and modernity. What a travesty if our scientific study of the Holocaust and its lessons should now, as we dare to approach the fire, produce nothing of moral and ethical and religious benefit to future generations! How tragic if the Holocaust should be nothing but a rather large footnote to ideas and responses already fixed and in place!

Elie Wiesel has been calling us again and again to contemplate silence, from the silence of God in *Night* [6] to the Prophet of Silence in *Twilight*. [7] It is the return to silence in the presence of the Story that stops trite explanations, stifles banal phrases, prevents premature closure, protects the sacred from the violence of profane hands, keeps the creative process open and clears space for the eternal generation of the Word of God.

Here too — as in liberating us to debate with God — Elie is respecting the sacredness of the memory, preserving the integrity of the Story, and opening a door toward the mending of the world.

NOTES

1. As related in Detroit, in "Some Religious Perspectives After Auschwitz," *The German Church Struggle and the Holocaust*, eds. Franklin H. Littell and Hubert G. Locke (Detroit: Wayne State University Press, 1974) 260-61. The story was originally published in "The Dean and the Chosen People," the second essay in Rubenstein's *After Auschwitz* (Indianapolis: Bobbs-Merrill Company, 1966).

2. Littell and Locke, Chapter 15.

3. See Harry James Cargas, ed. *Responses to Elie Wiesel* (New York: Persea Books, 1978) 283, 286.

4. Roberta Kalechofsky, *The 6th Day of Creation* (Marblehead, MA: Micah Publications, 1986) 5.

5. Thomas Mann, *Doctor Faustus* (New York: Vintage Books, 1948) 69.

6. Elie Wiesel, "I no longer accepted God's silence." *Night* (New York: Avon Books, 1969), PB of 1960 English translation, 80.

7. Elie Wiesel, "I am the prophet who chooses to be silent." *Twilight* (New York: Summit Books, 1987) 73.

RE-MEMBERING:
IN HONOR OF ELIE WIESEL

by DOROTHEE SOELLE

It is not easy to be German in this century, carrying the burden of collective shame and responsibility (as to be distinguished from guilt). I would like to introduce to you my generation of German intellectuals, writers and artists by recalling the haunting question under which we started our spiritual journey. It has been a question that took at least ten years of my young adulthood and will never leave me.

Today, living in a world of confused spiritual orphans, I sometimes feel that the legacy of this frightening and unanswerable quest has given us a certain advantage over the generation of young people wrestling with a thousand questions. We, who were fifteen when the war ended, had but three questions, and we went around asking our fathers and mothers, our teachers and professors, our textbooks and traditions these questions: "How could it have happened?"; "Were you there when it happened?"; "What did you do?"

The most terrifying responses we got to this questioning went like this: "We didn't know"; "We lived in a remote village"; "We had no Jewish friends"; "We heard rumors but never saw those things with our own eyes"; "We really did not know what was going on." They were not isolated responses. We heard them over and over again.

I guess I got my hands burned in touching those responses because I knew precisely that they were lies, those evasive, self-protecting lies people use to claim their innocence. They preferred to plunge into oblivion. Since the majority of decent Germans did not know what was happening at the time, why should they learn about it later? Who needs to remember anyhow?

During the controversy surrounding President Reagan's visit to

Previously unpublished, this tribute is printed by permission of the author.

the Bitburg military cemetery in 1985, Chancellor Kohl contended that he could not be held responsible for the events of 1933-45 on the basis of the "grace of being born too late" and thus having been too young to share responsibility. Mr. Kohl named this "die Gnade der spaeten Geburt" — an outrageous use of the theological concept of grace.

What "grace" is he talking about? Can there be a grace that never saw that night Elie Wiesel saw? Is grace to be restricted to the daylight only? My sense of this is that "God is memory," to borrow a phrase from process theology. In other words, to live in oblivion is to separate oneself from God. There is no grace in being born late. Grace shines through those who do remember, but living in the limbo of oblivion is to dis-member oneself from God.

Above all, I want to thank you, Elie Wiesel, for not letting the questions die, for telling the story. Thank you for reminding us and, in so doing, being a catalyst of a process of re-membering in the most literal sense of this word: making us into members of the human family again.

There are times when I doubt that it is possible to remember my German people into the human family. It is as though, as in the last phrase of Kafka's *The Trial*, there is a shame that even outlives K's shame. This companion of my sleepless nights — will it transform my days?

Shame, says another great Jewish thinker of the 19th century by the name of Karl Marx, is a revolutionary virtue. It leads beyond the status quo. Does it? Will it? The shame we were born with has transformed, in an essential way, the theologizing of at least some people of my generation. In deep indebtedness to all of your work, Elie, I would like to ponder with you the work of the playwright, particularly your "Trial of God." It is the story of the happening on February 25, 1649, in Schangorod, during the Chmielinicki pogrom in Russia.

At a small village inn a Purim play is presented, and three Purim actors perform a trial in which God is indicted because of the suffering of his children. The play takes place after the pogrom, but while the actors drink and celebrate the traditional feast in which "all is free" and things are told which no one dares to speak at other times, a gang of murderers gets together again outside the inn.

Precisely speaking, the play is played between two pogroms, and it deals with the theme of theodicy. The three drunken Purim players try to find an advocate for God — in vain! The prosecutor says:

> There is no defendant of God! So what? Whose failure is that? God has killed his advocates, has delivered them to the murderers. He did not spare the judge Jeb Schmouel, he did not preserve the life of the teacher Reb Baruch. Hirsch, the wise man, and Melech the shoemaker did love him, did believe in him, only in him! But he did not care for them. Whose fault is it that they keep silent? Whose fault is it then that they have become dust? Whose guilt is it when the earth is populated with murderers . . . with murderers only?

In the end of the play a stranger appears from the night, an ambivalent, beautiful and cold figure by the name of Sam. He is ready to play the role of the defendant of God. He affirms God's omnipotence and absoluteness. "I am his servant," he claims. "God has created the world and us without asking about our opinion. He can act as it pleases him. Our task is to glorify him nevertheless."

When the players finally put on their masks to begin the performance of the trial, Sam covers himself with the mask of the Devil and erupts into long, loud laughter. He gives a sign to those outside the inn, and the gang of killers enters.

The playwright takes the theme of theodicy more seriously than most theologians have done; they often get stuck in the position of being advocates for God. This seriousness expresses itself with grim humor when the parts of the play are cast. The three drunken Purim players are the judges. The daughter of the innkeeper, who went insane over gang rape, is the witness to the accusation. The old innkeeper, who is the most pious of all of them, becomes the most pitiless accusor. Ironically enough, the defendant is absent, as is his habit.

The glib theologian turns out to be Satan. He names himself a messenger of God: "I have been roaming all over the earth and have informed God. I see all and know all. I cannot create anything but can annihilate everything!"

One of the great strengths of Elie Wiesel's writing, for me, lies in his capacity to avoid the leap into a higher level, into a sort of meta-plan. The author of this play never allows us to neutralize the question; he never historicizes it. Do we have to accuse God? Can we defend God? Is there a defense of God that is not Satanic but comes out of a greater love for God? Or is the accusation the greatest gesture of love of God of which we are capable? In some of Elie Wiesel's figures it seems to be so.

Where then do theologians, who should narrate the great deeds of God and laud God's very being, belong in this play? More specifically, what has Christian theology to say?

I ask these questions after Auschwitz. I cannot, and will not, ask them such timeless questions. I cannot compare the earthquake in Lisbon in 1755 with the Holocaust of the Jews done by the Germans. My questions refer to Christian theology: "Where?"; "In which perspective?"; and "How does it have to change (after the *Shoah*)?"

These questions led at least some Christian theologians into a critical re-lecture of the New Testament and its anti-Judaistic tendencies. It led also to a rewriting of church history under the perspective of Christendom's relation to the Jewish people in different periods. Thirdly, these questions have consequences for systematic theological reflection and enforced revision of our concept of God. Elie Wiesel's writings have helped many of us to enter a process of working toward a more just vision of God.

Classical theodicy, as developed in the 17th and 18th centuries, tried to reconcile three qualities of the Godhead to each other: omnipotence, love, and comprehensibility. It is fair to summarize the outcome of the debate in stating that only two of the three theological statements are thinkable together; one in each solution has to be excluded.

(1) God is omnipotent and comprehensible but not loving. This concept poses God as the almighty ruler of history and of each individual's life. God stands, figuratively speaking, at the summit of the universe, as the great ruler, the one who knows everything, who is really responsible; the one who can, at least, step in and end human torment, assuming He wants to.

In this context, we often speak of the suffering of the innocent, of children who are tormented, for example. But in a deeper sense all human beings are innocent. No one deserves to starve. Not a single one of the six million who were gassed — even if he or she otherwise lied, stole or was a beast — ever "deserved" the suffering inflicted upon him or her. An almighty God who inflicts suffering, who looks down from above on Auschwitz, must be a sadist. And a theology which thinks up such a chief ruler, producer, a responsible originator and mastermind, reflects the sadism of its authors. "He" stands on the side of the victors. He is, to borrow the words of a black theologian, a "white racist."

In Elie Wiesel's play, this is the position of Satan. He appears always when murder occurs; he advocates submission. His God is sheer power, love being excluded.

(2) God is almighty and all-loving but at the same time *not* comprehensible. He withdraws from our understanding. Faith in this God becomes absurd or, at best, a paradox. But a mere paradoxical faith cannot be held onto — Soren Kierkegaard is proof of this.

(3) God is justice and love but not all-powerful. Between victors and victims, God is only trustworthy *if* God stands on the side of the victims and is capable of suffering. This position is held today by various Jewish thinkers like Emil Fackenheim, Abraham Heschel, Hans Jonas and Elie Wiesel. Even popular theologians, such as Rabbi Kushner (*When Bad Things Happen to Good People*), share this position.

For a Christian perspective, I recall Dietrich Bonhoeffer, who, while in a Nazi prison, came close to an understanding of a suffering God. I mentioned process theology, which articulates God's being in need of us and emphasizes God's becoming over God's being. I engage in theologies of liberation both in their Latin American and their feminist branches.

I want to speak of God's pain, "der Schmerz Gottes." I am not speaking of something which God could avoid or do away with. If we speak of God's pain, then we have another conception of God than a purely masculine one. This God is our mother, who weeps over the things that we do to each other and to our sisters and brothers, the animals and plants. God comforts us like a mother. She cannot make the pain go away by magic (although that occasionally happens too!), but she holds us in her lap until we stand up again with renewed strength.

God could not comfort us if she were not connected to us in pain, if she did not have this wonderful and rare ability to feel another's pain in her own body. To have compassion means to suffer with, to be present with. If you allow me to refer to the religious traditions I grew up with, the Gospels describe Jesus as one who has this ability. If he is there when someone is slapped in the face, he winces and feels the blow on his own cheek. If someone is lied to, he is there with his need for truth. If a whole people is trampled down by the brutal might of the empire, he weeps over his city, Jerusalem.

I have just said, in a realistic and limited way, "If he is there when these things happen." But now let us try to think of God, and we can remove this limitation. *All* who suffer are in the presence of God. There is no longer an "if." God does not forget!

The *praesentia Dei* is not a mere observing presence but is always the pain or joy of God. Without God's pain, God is not really present, but only turns up from time to time like a president who occasionally visits the people. But God takes part in our suffering.

I would like to thank you, Elie Wiesel, for re-connecting me with God's pain. May I say that you have helped me to move from my national identity of shame, and at times of despair, into partaking in God's pain.

If one thinks of us being God's children, growing finally up into God's adult children, we may understand ourselves as people of God who participate in God's life of joy and sorrow. Yet we remember history so that we can get out of this everlasting circle of repeating oppression and subjugation. To remember who we were and what we did, then, would mean that God re-members us — in the double sense of the words.

I understand your writing, Elie, as a prayer to God to end the numbing and to free the alienated humans — who have been dis-membered for so long.

May God re-member all of us!

FROM *NIGHT* TO *TWILIGHT*:
A PHILOSOPHER'S READING OF ELIE WIESEL

by JOHN K. ROTH

> *Everything to do with Auschwitz must, in the end, lead into darkness.*
> — Elie Wiesel

Plato and Aristotle, Hume and Kant, Hegel and Kierkegaard, James, Camus and Wittgenstein — these great masters of philosophy move me. Philosophically, however, no writer disturbs and provokes me more than one who claims he "never intended to be a philosopher."[1] Whenever I read a book by Elie Wiesel, survivor of the Holocaust, the Nazi attempt to annihilate the Jews, I feel compelled to respond in writing of my own. No other author affects me quite that way.

For nearly thirty years I have been doing a philosopher's reading of Elie Wiesel. On this occasion I write because I have just reread, as I do annually, his first book, *La Nuit* (1958; translated as *Night*, 1960), and also because his novel *Le Crepuscule, au loin* (1987; translated as *Twilight*, 1988) has been on my mind. *Twilight* complements, not to say completes, a quest begun with *Night* and incorporates everything else that Wiesel has written in between.

THE DOMAIN OF MADNESS

Speaking of *Night*, that classic memoir about his entry into and exodus from Auschwitz, Wiesel has said "all my subsequent books are built around it."[2] Spare and lean, that book starts with a boy who "believed profoundly." It ends with a reflection: "From the depths of the mirror, a corpse gazed back at me. The look in his eyes, as they stared into mine, has never left me."[3] In *l'univers concentrationnaire*, as another Holocaust survivor, David Rousset,

This essay is based on a paper presented at a symposium held at Webster University, St. Louis, Missouri, on September 29, 1988. A revised version appeared in *Religion & Literature* 24.1 (Spring 1992): pp. 59-73. It is printed by permission of the author.

named it, assumptions treasured and persons loved were stripped away. But the dead left Wiesel behind to wonder and thereby to encounter the living.

L'Aube (1960; translated as Dawn, 1961) is Wiesel's second major work. This brief novel portrays Elisha, a young Holocaust survivor who strives to free Palestine from British rule so that a people and a nation can find new life. This, Elisha discovers, is easier said than done. Once the possible victim of an executioner, he must execute a British captain, John Dawson, in retribution for the slaying of an Israeli freedom fighter. "That's it," Elisha says to himself. "It's done. I've killed. I've killed Elisha." Insofar as choosing life requires choosing death as well, dawn may be difficult to distinguish from "the tattered fragment of darkness" that reflects Elisha's face as he gazes through a window at the breaking of a not-so-new day.[4]

Hitler's "final solution" still seems to mock quests for healing resolutions. Thus, Dawn's title is ironic, for after Auschwitz, despair coils like a serpent in the heart of being. In Wiesel's third book, Le Jour (1961; translated not literally as "Day" but as The Accident, 1962), despite the fact that he has friends and even a woman who loves him, another suvivor, Eliezer, steps in front of a moving car. The "accident" is no accident, yet life returns to be chosen again. "The problem," Wiesel proposes, "is not: to be or not to be. But rather: to be and not to be."[5] But how best to do so? Wiesel turns to that question again and again.

In The Accident, the victim's artist-friend, Gyula, whose name means redemption, urges Eliezer to choose life and put the past behind him. He paints Eliezer's portrait. The eyes are searing since "they belonged to a man who had seen God commit the most unforgivable crime: to kill without a reason." After showing Eliezer the portrait, Gyula symbolizes the end of the past by setting fire to the canvas. Though he is moved by Gyula's testimony, Eliezer will not be fully healed by it, for the novel's final line states that Gyula departed and forgot "to take along the ashes."[6]

Moving through night into dawn and day, Elie Wiesel's first works travel through the destruction of a supportive universe into a post-Holocaust world of ambiguity and nothingness in which life almost succeeds in fulfilling a desire to cancel itself. Plumbing such depths had to be the prelude to Wiesel's hard-won insistence that the essence of being Jewish is "never to give up — never to yield to despair."[7] That affirmation is one of his categorical imperatives.

Keeping it is anything but easy, as *Twilight* shows. Its story does so by asking about "the domain of madness," a realm never far from the center of Wiesel's consciousness. By illuminating, in particular, Maimonides' conviction that "the world couldn't exist without madmen"[8] — it serves as the novel's epigraph — *Twilight* also has much to say about friendship.

FRIENDSHIP

Arguably Wiesel's most complex novel, *Twilight* defies simple summary. One of its dominant themes emerges, however, when Raphael Lipkin's telephone rings at midnight. This survivor of the Holocaust, now a university scholar, hears an anonymous voice denouncing his friend, Pedro: "Professor, let me tell you about your friend, Pedro. He is totally amoral. A sadist. He made me suffer. And not just me, there were many others."[9] Pedro is Raphael's friend indeed. More than once he saved Raphael from the despair that repeatedly threatens to engulf him. Pedro's help has been more than physical. He taught the young Lipkin, "It may not be in man's power to erase society's evil, but he must become its conscience; it may not be in his power to create the glories of the night, but he must wait for them and describe their beauty."[10]

The midnight calls keep calling Pedro into question and Raphael into despair. Madness lies in waiting, and, if Pedro were destroyed, Raphael might succumb to it. Recognition of that possibility, recollection that "Pedro taught me to love mankind and celebrate its humanity despite its flaws," renewed realization that Pedro's "enemy is my enemy" — such forces rally Raphael's resistance.[11] By reaffirming a summons to save, Raphael's battle against madness that destroys does not ensure a tranquil equilibrium. A different kind of madness, the moral madness without which the world could not exist, is the prospect instead. "The caller tried to drive you out of my life," Raphael tells the absent Pedro. "He failed. Does that mean I've won? Hardly. I cry into the night and the night does not answer. Never mind, I will shout and shout until I go deaf, until I go mad."[12]

Twilight is not the first time a man named Pedro has appeared in Wiesel's novels and provided saving inspiration. Differing from his namesake in *Twilight* because he is not Jewish, another Pedro is a decisive presence in *La Ville de la chance* (1962; translated as *The*

Town Beyond the Wall). This book, Wiesel's fourth and fittingly the one most closely linked to *Twilight*, begins with an epigraph from Dostoevsky: "I have a plan — to go mad."[13] It also starts at twilight and under circumstances that can drive one to madness that destroys.

Once Michael's home, Szerencsevaros ("the city of luck") is in the vise of Communist victors over Nazi tryrants. Secretly returning to see whether anyone can be found, Michael stands before his former home. Ages ago a face watched silently there while Jews were sent away. The face, seeking a hatred from Michael to match its own hidden guilt, informs the police. Michael finds himself imprisoned in walls within his past, tortured to tell a story that cannot be told. There is no political plot to reveal; his captors would never accept the simple truth of his desire to see his hometown once more; his friend, Pedro, who returned with him, must be protected.

Michael holds out. He resists an escape into one kind of madness by opening himself to another. His cellmate, Eliezer, dwells in catatonic silence. But Michael hears and heeds the advice that he knows his friend Pedro would give him: "That's exactly what I want you to do: recreate the universe. Restore that boy's sanity. Cure him. He'll save you."[14]

What of such a plan? *Twilight*, as well as *The Town Beyond the Wall* and some thirty more of Wiesel's books, follows *Night*. In one way or another, all of *Night*'s sequels explore how the world might be mended. Nonetheless in the order of things, dawn, day, and especially twilight leave night close by. Yet even if, as Wiesel contends, "everything to do with Auschwitz must, in the end, lead into darkness," questions remain concerning what that darkness might be and whether the leading into darkness is indeed the end. For if *The Town Beyond the Wall* concludes with Michael's coming "to the end of his strength," it also ends with "the night . . . receding, as on a mountain before dawn."[15] Similarly, as *Twilight* moves toward night, "from far away, a star appears. Uncommonly brilliant."[16]

Twilight and *The Town Beyond the Wall* are both novels about friendship, another theme that is never far from the center of Wiesel's vision. Both Michael and Raphael have friends named Pedro. In each case, Pedro serves as a special kind of teacher. These relationships transcend the physical limits of space and time. Even when absent from *The Town Beyond the Wall* or from *Twilight*, the two Pedros are very much present for their friends. Michael and Raphael take courage from the challenging encouragement that each one's

Pedro provides.

Michael and Raphael have learned from their friends Pedro. What they have discerned resonates with lessons I am trying to learn as I pursue a philosopher's reading of Elie Wiesel. Let us consider the authorship that moves from *Night* to *Twilight*, with journeys to *The Town Beyond the Wall* and meetings with Pedro among the multitude of encounters in between, reflect on ten of his major insights — two sets of five that focus first on understanding and then on doing. Simple and yet complex, complex and yet simple, each point is central, I believe, to Wiesel's way of thinking and living and to his expression of friendship in particular. None of the insights is an abstract principle; all are forged in fire that threatens to consume. For these reasons these themes from Wiesel have integrity, credibility, and durability that make them worthy guidelines for all seasons.

UNDERSTANDING

Elie Wiesel seeks understanding — but not too much. While wanting people to study the Holocaust, he alerts them to the dangers of thinking that they do or can or even should know everything about it. While wanting people to meet as friends, he cautions that such meetings will be less than honest if differences are glossed over, minimized, or forgotten.

While wanting humankind and God to confront each other, he contends that easy acceptance is at once too much and too little to accept. Wiesel's understanding is not facile, not obvious, nor automatic. Nevertheless its rhythm can be learned. Five of its movements follow.

1. *"The Holocaust demands interrogation and calls everything into question. Traditional ideas and acquired values, philosophical systems and social theories — all must be revised in the shadow of Birkenau."*[17] Birkenau was the killing center of Auschwitz, and the first lesson Wiesel teaches is that the Holocaust is an unrivaled measure because nothing exceeds its power to evoke the question "Why?" That authority puts everything else to the test.

Whatever the traditional ideas and acquired values that have existed, whatever the philosophical systems and social theories that human minds have produced, they were either inadequate to prevent Auschwitz, or, worse, they helped pave the way to that place. The Holocaust insists, therefore, that how we think and act need revision in the face of those facts unless one wishes to continue the same blindness that eventuated in the darkness of *Night*. The needed revisions, of course, do not guarantee a better outcome. Yet failure to use the Holocaust to call each other, and especially ourselves, into question diminishes chances to mend the world.

2. *"The questions remain questions."*[18] As the first lesson suggests, Elie Wiesel does not place his greatest confidence in answers. Answers — especially when they take the form of philosophical and theological systems — make him suspicious. No matter how hard people try to resolve the most important issues, questions remain and rightly so. To encounter the Holocaust, to reckon with its disturbing "Why?"s — without which our humanity itself is called into question — that is enough to make Wiesel's case.

Typically, however, the human propensity is to quest for certainty. Wiesel's urging is to resist that temptation, especially when it aims to settle things that ought to remain unsettled and unsettling. For if answers aim to settle things, their ironic, even tragic, outcome is often that they produce disagreement, division, and death. Hence, Wiesel wants questions to be forever fundamental.

People are less likely to savage and annihilate each other when their minds are not made up but opened up through questioning. The Holocaust shows as much: Hitler and his Nazi followers "knew" they were "right." Their "knowing" made them killers. Questioning might have redeemed them as well as their victims.

Wiesel's point is not that responses to questions are simply wrong. They have their place; they can be essential, too. Nevertheless, questions deserve lasting priority because they invite continuing inquiry, further dialogue, shared wonder, and openness. Resisting final solutions, these ingredients — especially when they drive home the insight that the best questions are never put to rest but keep us human by luring us on — can create friendships in ways that answers never can.

3. *"And yet — and yet. This is the key expression in my work."*[19] Elie Wiesel's writings, emerging from intensity that is both the burden and the responsibility of Holocaust survivors, aim to put people off guard. Always suspicious of answers but never failing for questions, he lays out problems not for their own sake but to inquire, "What is the next step?" Reaching an apparent conclusion, he moves on.

Such forms of thought reject easy paths in favor of hard ones.

Wiesel's "and yet — and yet" affirms that it is more important to seek than to find, more important to question than to answer, more important to travel than to arrive. The point is that it can be dangerous to believe what you want to believe, deceptive to find things too clear, just as it is also dishonest not to strive to bring them into focus. His caution is that it is insensitive to overlook that there is always more to experience than our theories admit, even though we can never begin to seek comprehension without reasoning and argument. So Elie Wiesel tells his stories, and even their endings resist leaving his readers with a fixed conclusion. He wants them instead to feel his "and yet — and yet," which provides a hope that people may keep moving to choose life and not to end it.

4. *"There is a link between language and life."*[20] The Holocaust was physically brutal. That brutality's origins were partly in "paper violence," which is to say that they depended on words. Laws, decrees, orders, memoranda, even schedules for trains and specifications for gas vans and crematoria — all of these underwrite Wiesel's insistence that care must be taken with words, for words can kill.

Wiesel uses words differently. He speaks and writes to recreate. His words, including the silences they contain, bring forgotten places and unremembered victims back to life just as they jar the living from complacency. Doing these things, he understands, requires turning language against itself. During the Nazi era, language hid too much. Euphemisms masked reality to lull. Rhetoric projected illusions to captivate. Propaganda used lies to control. All of those efforts were hideously successful. In our own day, as Wiesel points out, we bid farewell by saying, "Relax," "Have fun," "Take it easy." Seemingly innocuous, such language is certainly a far cry from words possessed by genocidal intent. Yet innocuous words may not be as innocent as they seem. They are likely to distract and detract from needs that deserve concern and care.

Language and life are linked in more ways than words can say. Post-Auschwitz priorities nonetheless enjoin that words have to decode words, speech must say what speech hides, writing must rewrite and set right what has been written. None of this can be done perfectly, once and for all. The task is ongoing, but only as it is going on will lives be linked so that "and yet — and yet" expresses hope more than despair.

5. *"Rationalism is a failure and betrayal."*[21] Although Elie Wiesel is hardly an enemy of reason and rationality, he does stand with philosophers who believe that one of reason's most important functions is to assess its own limitations. Yet Wiesel's critique of reason is grounded somewhat differently from David Hume's or Immanuel Kant's. Theirs depends on theory. Wiesel's rests on history and on the Holocaust in particular.

The Holocaust happened because human minds became convinced that they could figure everything out. Those minds "understood" that one religion had superseded another. They "comprehended" that one race was superior to every other. They "realized" who deserved to live and who deserved to die. One can argue, of course, that such views undermined rationality and perverted morality. They did. But to say that much is too little, for one must ask about the sources of those outcomes. When that asking occurs, part of its trail leads to reason's tendency to presume that indeed it can, at least in principle, figure everything out.

With greater authority than any theory can muster, Auschwitz shows where such rationalism can lead. Wiesel's antidote is not irrationalism; his rejection of destructive madness testifies to that. What he seeks instead is the understanding that lives in friendship, understanding that includes tentativeness, fallibility, comprehension that looks for error and revises judgment when error is found, realization that knowing is not a matter of fixed conviction but of continuing dialogue.

DOING

Elie Wiesel's lessons about understanding urge one not to draw hasty or final conclusions. Rather his emphasis is on exploration and inquiry. It might be said that such an outlook tends to encourage indecision and even indifference. To the contrary, however, one of Wiesel's most significant philosophical contributions runs in just the opposite direction. His perspective on understanding and on morality is of one piece. Thus, dialogue leads not to indecision but to an informed decisiveness. Tentativeness becomes protest when unjustified conviction asserts itself. Openness results not in indifference but in the loyalty of which friendship is made and on which it depends. Wiesel's doing is demanding, but it, too, has a rhythm that can be learned. Here are five of its movements.

1. *"Passivity and indifference and neutrality always favor the killer, not the victim."*[22] Elie Wiesel will never fully understand the world's killers. To do so would be to legitimatize them by showing that they were part of a perfectly rational scheme. Though for very different reasons, he will not fully understand their victims, either; their silent screams call into question every account of their dying that presents itself as a final solution.

Wiesel insists that understanding should be no less elusive where indifference — including its accomplices, passivity and neutrality — prevails. Too often indifference exists among those who could make a difference, for it can characterize those who stand between killers and victims but aid the former against the latter by doing too little, too late. Where acting is concerned, nothing arouses Wiesel more than activating the inactive.

2. *"It is given to man to transform divine injustice into human justice and compassion."*[23] Abraham and Isaac, Moses, and Job — these "messengers of God," as Wiesel calls them, understood that men and women abuse the freedom to choose, which makes life human. They also wrestled with the fact that human existence neither accounts for nor completely sustains itself. Their dearly-earned reckoning with that reality led them to a profound restiveness. It revealed, in turn, the awesome injunction that God intends for humankind to have hard, even impossible, moral work until and through death.

One may not see life the way those biblical messengers saw it. Whatever one's choices in that regard, it is nevertheless as hard as it is inhuman to deny that injustice too often reigns divine and that moral work is given to us indeed. Elie Wiesel presumes neither to identify that work in detail for everyone nor to insist, in particular, where or how one should do it. Those are the right questions, though, and he wants one to explore them. That exploration, he urges, is not likely to be done better than through Holocaust lenses. Enhancing vision sensitively, they can help to focus every evil that should be transformed by human justice and compassion.

3. *"If I still shout today, if I still scream, it is to prevent man from ultimately changing me."*[24] While "and yet — and yet" may be the key expression in Wiesel's writings, a close contender could be phrased "because of — in spite of." Here, too, the rhythm insists that, no matter where one dwells, there is and must be more to say and do. On this occasion, though, the context is more specific, for the place

where "because of — in spite of" becomes crucial is the place where despair most threatens to win. So, because of the odds in favor of despair and against hope, in spite of them, the insistence and need to rebel in favor of life are all the greater. And not to be moved by them is to hasten the end. How this logic works is reflected in a story that Wiesel often tells. A Just Man came to Sodom to save that ill-fated place from sin and destruction. A child, observing the Just Man's care, approached him compassionately:

"Poor stranger, you shout, you scream, don't you see that it is hopeless?"

"Yes, I see."

"Then why do you go on?"

"I'll tell you why. In the beginning, I thought I could change man. Today, I know I cannot. If I still shout today, if I still scream, it is to prevent man from ultimately changing me."

The Just Man's choice is one that others can make as well. Thus, a future still awaits our determination, especially if the rhythm "because of — in spite of" is understood and enacted.

4. *"As a Jew I abide by my tradition. And my tradition allows, and indeed commands, man to take the Almighty to task for what is being done to His people, to His children — and all men are His children — provided the questioner does so on behalf of His children, not against them, from within the community, from within the human condition, and not as an outsider."*[25] Some of Elie Wiesel's most forceful writing involves the Jewish tradition know as Hasidism. [26] Many features impress him as he traces this movement from its flowering in eighteenth-century Europe, to its presence in the death camps, and to its continuing influence in a world that came close to annihilating Hasidic ways root and branch. One of the rhythms of understanding and doing stressed by Wiesel derives, at least in part, from a Hasidic awareness of the relationships between "being for — being against."

Hasidism, in particular, combines a genuine awe of God with direct and emotional reactions toward God. It finds God eluding understanding but also as One to whom people can speak. The Hasidic masters argue with God, protest against God, fear, trust, and love God. All of this is done personally and passionately, without compromising God's majesty and beyond fear of contradiction. Levi-Yitzhak of Berditchev, for example, understood his role as that of attorney-for-the-defense, reproaching God for harsh treatment the Jews received. Joining him was Rebbe Israel, Maggid of Kozhenitz, author of one of Wiesel's favorite Hasidic prayers: "Master of the Universe, know that the children of Israel are suffering too much; they deserve redemption, they need it. But if, for reasons unknown to me, You are not willing, not yet, then redeem all the other nations, but do it soon!"[27]

Nahman of Bratzlav holds another special place in Wiesel's heart. Laughter is Nahman's gift:

> Laughter that springs from lucid and desperate aware-
> ness, a mirthless laughter, laughter of protest against the
> absurdities of existence, a laughter of revolt against a
> universe where man, whatever he may do, is condemned
> in advance. A laughter of compassion for man who
> cannot escape the ambiguity of his condition and of his
> faith.[28]

And a final example, Menahem-Mendl of Kotzk, embodied a spirit whose intense despair yielded righteous anger and revolt so strong that it was said, "a God whose intentions he would understand could not suit him."[29] This rebel embraced life's contradictions both to destroy and to sustain them. Short of death, he found life without release from suffering. At the same time, he affirmed humanity as precious by living defiantly to the end. Wiesel implies, too, that Mendl hoped for something beyond death. His final words, Wiesel suggests, were "At last I shall see Him face to face." Wiesel adds, "We don't know — nor will we ever know — whether these words expressed an ancient fear or a renewed defiance."[30]

Anything can be said and done, indeed everything *must* be said and done, that is *for* men and women. Wiesel understands this to mean that a stance against God is sometimes enjoined. But he hastens to add that such a stance needs to be from within a perspective that also affirms God. Otherwise we run the risk of being against humankind in other ways all over again. Those ways include succumbing to dehumanizing temptations which conclude that only human might makes right, that there is human history as we know it and nothing more, and that, as far as the Holocaust's victims are concerned, Hitler was victorious.

For . . . against: that rhythm involves taking stands. Spiritually this means to be against God when being for God would put one against mankind. Spiritually this also means to be for God when

being against God would put one against humankind by siding
with forces that tend, however inadvertently, to legitimize too
much the wasting of human life. Elie Wiesel is fiercely humanistic.
His humanism, however, remains tied to God. The lesson here is
that without enlivening and testing those ties and, in particular,
their ways of being for and against humankind, a critical resource
for saving life and mending the world will be lost.

    5. *"By allowing me to enter his life, he gave meaning to mine."*[31] Elie
Wiesel's 1973 novel, *Le Serment de Kolvillage* (*The Oath*), tells of a
community that disappeared except for one surviving witness. It is
a tale about that person's battle with a vow of silence. Azriel is his
name, and Kolvillag, his home in eastern Europe, was destroyed in
a twentieth-century pogrom prompted by the disappearance of a
Christian boy. Ancient animosity renewed prejudice; prejudice
produced rumor; rumor inflamed hate. Accused of a ritual murder,
Azriel and his fellow Jews were soon under threat.

    Moché, a strange, mystical member of the community, surren-
ders himself as the guilty party though no crime has been committed.
But he does not satisfy the authorities and "Christians" of the town.
Madness intensifies. The Jews begin to see that history will repeat,
and they prepare for the worst. Some arm for violence; most gather
strength quietly to wait and endure.

    Permitted to speak to the Jews assembled in their ancient
synagogue, Moché envisions Kolvillag's destruction. He knows
the record of Jewish endurance, its long testimony against violence,
but this seems to have done little to restrain men and women and
even God from further vengeance. So Moché persuades his people
to try something different: "By ceasing to refer to the events of the
present, we would forestall ordeals in the future."[32] The Jews of
Kolvillag become Jews of silence by taking his oath: "Those among
us who will survive this present ordeal shall never reveal either in
writing or by the word what we shall see, hear and endure before
and during our torment."[33]

    Next comes bloodshed. Jewish spirits strain upward in smoke
and fire. Only the young Azriel survives. He bears the chronicles of
Kolvillag, one created with his eyes, the other in a book entrusted
to him for safekeeping by his father, the community's historian.
Azriel bears the oath of Kolvillag as well. Torn between speech and
silence, he remains true to his promise.

    Many years later, Azriel meets a young man who is about to kill himself in a desperate attempt to give his life significance by refusing to live it. Azriel decides to intervene, to find a way to make the waste of suicide impossible for his new friend. The way Azriel chooses entails breaking the oath. He shares the story of Kolvillag in the hope that it will instill rebellion against despair, concern in the place of lethargy and indifference, life to counter death.

The oath of silence was intended to forestall ordeals in the future. Such forestalling, Wiesel testifies, must give silence its due; it must also break silence in favor of speech and action that recognizes the ultimate interdependence of existence. "By allowing me to enter his life, he gave meaning to mine." Azriel's young friend echoes and sums up the insights that Elie Wiesel has shared so generously with those who have read carefully what he has to say. Rightly understood, that understanding becomes a mandate for doing unto others what Azriel does for the boy he saves.

REMEMBERING

As I studied *Twilight* for this essay, I was also rereading an earlier book called *Axis Rule in Occupied Europe*. If the name of its author was not on Wiesel's mind when he wrote *Twilight*, it did keep running through mine as I traced the odyssey of Wiesel's character, Raphael Lipkin.

Originally published in 1944, *Axis Rule in Occupied Europe* was written by a Jewish legal scholar named Raphael Lemkin (1901-1959). A resident of Warsaw, Poland, he was wounded during guerrilla fighting outside Warsaw while resisting the German invasion of his homeland in 1939. After weeks of hiding in Polish forests, Lemkin escaped to Sweden by way of Lithuania and the Baltic Sea. There he began to document the Nazis' murderous policies, policies that, at the war's end, would leave him as the sole survivor among some forty of his closest family members.

In 1941 Lemkin found his way to the United States. He taught with distinction at Duke, Yale, Rutgers, and Princeton, and he helped to prepare cases against Nazis who stood trial in Nuremberg after the Second World War. While still at Duke, he published *Axis Rule in Occupied Europe*. In its pages he defined a term he had coined —genocide—as he attempted to fathom, while it was still happening, what is now called the Holocaust or *Shoah*. Four years later, in 1948, Lemkin's leadership was instrumental in obtaining passage for the

United Nations' Genocide Convention. These efforts made him a strong contender for the 1950 Nobel Peace Prize.

Like Wiesel's men named Pedro, Lemkin was not without detractors. Some called him a dreamer, others a fanatic. A more apt description makes him a brother to Wiesel's morally sensitive madmen. Like Raphael Lipkin and his creator, Elie Wiesel, Raphael Lemkin worked to forestall ordeals in the future. Thus, it is fitting that the name Raphael links not only the three of them but all who have been and will be touched by the lessons that reading Wiesel has to teach.

Some ancient texts — Tobit, for example, and Enoch — as well as kabbalistic writings refer to an angel named Raphael. Stories about this angel make clear that Raphael has power to conquer demons. The name, significantly, is a compound of the Hebrew *rapha*, meaning "healed," and *El*, which designates God. Raphael, then, is the Angel of Healing or "God's healing."

After Auschwitz, divine powers of that kind may be found wanting, thus making human counterparts to the angelic Raphael all the more important. Without them, God's healing, in all of its varied nuances, may not exist. To conquer demons permanently and forever — that task is more than human energy can accomplish. Nevertheless, to resist them and to apply a healing touch wherever and whenever the opportunity arises — that Raphael-like task is one that cannot be shirked with impunity.

If reading from *Night* to *Twilight* drives home Elie Wiesel's insights about understanding and doing, it will still be true that "everything to do with Auschwitz must, in the end, lead into darkness." Nevertheless, that end ought not to be the ending. Remembering and acting accordingly could lead beyond. Honesty probably permits no greater optimism in the twilight that forms the post-Holocaust world. And yet some light remains. Though not as much as we need, might it be enough to keep destruction's nighttime madness at bay so that day can dawn again?

NOTES

1. Elie Wiesel, "Why I Write,"*Confronting the Holocaust: The Impact of Elie Wiesel*, trans. Rosette C. Lamont, eds. Alvin Rosenfeld and Irving Greenberg (Bloomington: Indiana University Press, 1978) 200. The quotation that serves as this article's epigraph is from "Auschwitz — Another Planet," Elie Wiesel's review of *Auschwitz* by Bernd Naumann. The review first appeared in *Hadassah Magazine* (January 1967) and is reprinted in Irving Abrahamson, ed., *Against Silence: The Voice and Vision of Elie Wiesel*, 3 vols. (New York:

Holocaust Library, 1985) 2: 293.

2. Elie Wiesel, "Talking and Writing and Keeping Silent," *The German Church Struggle and the Holocaust*, eds. Franklin H. Littell and Hubert G. Locke (Detroit: Wayne State University Press, 1974) 269.

3. Elie Wiesel, *Night*, trans. Stella Rodway (New York: Bantam Books, 1986) 1, 109.

4. Elie Wiesel, *Dawn*, trans. Frances Frenaye (New York: Avon Books, 1970) 126-27.

5. Elie Wiesel, *The Accident*, trans. Anne Borchardt (New York: Avon Books, 1970) 81.

6. Wiesel, *The Accident* 123, 127.

7. Elie Wiesel, *A Jew Today*, trans. Marion Wiesel (New York: Random House, 1978) 164. This work was published originally as *Un Juif aujourd'hui* in 1977.

8. Elie Wiesel, *Twilight*, trans. Marion Wiesel (New York: Summit Books, 1988) 202, 9.

9. Wiesel, *Twilight* 179.

10. Wiesel, *Twilight* 118.

11. Wiesel, *Twilight* 201.

12. Wiesel, *Twilight* 202.

13. See Elie Wiesel, *The Town Beyond the Wall*, trans. Stephen Becker (New York: Avon Books, 1970) 3.

14. Wiesel, *The Town* 182.

15. Wiesel, *The Town* 189.

16. Wiesel, *Twilight* 217.

17. Elie Wiesel, "Foreword," *Shadows of Auschwitz: A Christian Response to the Holocaust*, by Harry James Cargas (New York: Crossroad, 1990) ix.

18. Elie Wiesel, "Telling the Tale," *Against Silence: The Voice and Vision of Elie Wiesel*, ed. and comp. Irving Abrahamson, 3 vols. (New York: Holocaust Library) 1: 234. This text is from an address to the 49th General Assembly of the Union of Hebrew Congregations, November 1967.

19. Elie Wiesel, "Exile and the Human Condition," *Against Silence* 1: 183. This text is from a lecture to the International Young Presidents Organization, Madrid, Spain, April 1980.

20. Elie Wiesel, "Exile" 1: 182.

21. Elie Wiesel, "The Use of Words and the Weight of Silence," *Against Silence* 2: 79. This text is from an interview conducted by Lily Edelman, which appeared in the *National Jewish Monthly*, November 1973.

22. Elie Wiesel, "Freedom of Conscience — A Jewish Commentary," *Against Silence* 1: 210. This text is from an address at the Bicentennial Conference on Religious Liberty, Philadelphia, 27 April 1976.

23. Elie Wiesel, *Messengers of God: Biblical Portraits and Legends*, trans. Marion Wiesel (New York: Random House, 1976) 235. This work was published originally as *Celebration biblique: Portraits et legendes* in 1975.

24. Elie Wiesel, *One Generation After*, trans. Lily Edelman and Elie Wiesel (New York: Avon Books, 1972) 95. This work was published originally as *Entre deux soleils* in 1970. See also Elie Wiesel, *The Testament*, trans. Marion Wiesel (New York: Summit Books, 1981) 9. This novel was published originally as *Le Testament d'un poete juif assassine* in 1980.

25. Elie Wiesel, "The Trial of Man," *Against Silence* 1: 176. The text is from a lecture at Loyola University, Chicago, which Wiesel delivered on 12 April 1980.

26. See, for example, Elie Wiesel's *Souls on Fire: Portraits and Legends of Hasidic Masters*, trans. Marion Wiesel (New York: Random House, 1972); *Four Hasidic Masters and Their Struggle Against Melancholy* (Notre Dame, IN: University of Notre Dame Press, 1978); *Somewhere a Master: Further Hasidic Portraits and Legends*, trans. Marion Wiesel (New York: Summit Books, 1982); and *Sages and Dreamers: Biblical, Talmudic, and Hasidic Portraits and Legends*, trans. Marion Wiesel (New York: Summit Books, 1991). *Souls on Fire* was published originally as *Celebration hassidique: Portraits et legendes* in 1972. *Somewhere a Master* was published originally as *Contre la melancolie: Celebration hassidique II* in 1981.

27. Elie Wiesel, *Souls on Fire* 133.

28. Wiesel, *Souls* 198.

29. Wiesel, *Souls* 245.

30. Wiesel, *Souls* 254.

31. Elie Wiesel, *The Oath*, trans. Marion Wiesel (New York: Random House, 1973) 16. This novel was published originally as *Le Serment de Kolvillag* in 1973.

32. Wiesel, *The Oath* 239.

33. Wiesel, *The Oath* 241.

When an Eye Says Kaddish

by ELIE WIESEL

In memory of my murdered father

A Jew stands on his knees, and with his nails he digs a grave for himself and his brothers. His face is lost in darkness. One can barely see it. It is shrouded in eternal night. Arms folded, feet apart, a dozen German soldiers stand behind him. They are laughing.

A yellow Star of David on her breast, an old, broken grandmother stands at a train station somewhere in Poland. Like a cursed snake that swallows all light, a shadow looks out from her countenance. The Germans stand behind her. We do not see them. But we hear their laughter.

A dead man lies somewhere in Germany. He has covered his own face with his jacket as if out of shame for the Creation. He has died at his work. He has not endured it. He lies among stones, his right hand clenched in a fist. Take a good look at his feet. His right shoe has disappeared. Perhaps the dead man had only one shoe for two feet — and that is why he is gone.

We Have Not Forgotten is the name of a picture album recently published by the Polish government. The book contains over 250 pages. They portray a drop of the blood that the German "bearers of culture" spilled in Poland during the Second World War. I know that sleepless nights and bleak, frozen mornings await me.

I know that every eye that looks out at me from these photos will cut another branch from my tree and put another stain on the sun.

And yet the finger turns page after page, further and further, though a bizarre terror clutches the heart: a moment more, and I shall encounter myself.

I pause on each page, at each photo, in order to catch my breath. And I tell myself: nothing more terrifying can be shown, nothing

Written in 1960, this essay originally appeared in the *Jewish Daily Forward* and was translated from the Yiddish by Irving Abrahamson. It is printed by permission of the author.

worse can be invented. A minute later I am ashamed of myself: I have underestimated the murder fantasy of the superior German race.

Some sort of masochistic power drives me to hold open the mirror of the past eternity. The heart begs for the suffering of Job. I want to say Kaddish, not with the tongue — it has sinned too much with the word — only with the eye. In our generation one can no longer say Kaddish with the tongue. It is silent when it should not be, and it speaks when it should not. Perhaps only the eye contains enough purity and true pity to compel for the Creator a Kaddish that He has earned.

It is the eighteenth day of the month of Shevat.

Fifteen years ago today, my father, like the Prophet Elijah, rose up to heaven on a fiery chariot harnessed to fiery horses.

Since then I say Kaddish — more than one day a year.

* * *

A peculiar, quiet despair is poured across the profile of the *ka-tzetnik*, the concentration camp prisoner. Half sitting, he has thrown his belt in a noose around his neck and hanged himself from a pipe. He was unable to find a more suitable place on the entire earth to do this than in a toilet.

In that moment this dirty place was transformed into a courtroom where the suicide carried out a death sentence against mankind.

A grey sky. Five or six old men fall to the ground, cut down like wheat. A little further, a mother clasps her child to her breast in order to shield it with her own body. Behind her a German soldier aims his rifle. The mother falls and falls and falls.

Children with the swollen heads of old men; old men with the emaciated bodies of children. Pregnant women hang and stir the wind.

And the eye is not full. And the finger is not numb. Only more and more. Only a curse Kaddish is born on the lips. It seems to me that it will choke me if I do not spit it out on the peoples of the earth. A beautiful little Jewish boy, his hands in the air, a grownup's despair on his frightened little face. His cap is too big for him, and it falls low over his forehead. His eyes — two extinguished fires. German soldiers surround him, armed from head to toe. Dozens, hundreds, thousands of Germans, with rifles and machine guns, drive the shy little boy to his death. From one side the mighty

German army, from the other a Jewish *cheder* boy with the anguish of generations on the pallor of his face.

Go say Kaddish!

A scene from the Warsaw Ghetto uprising: a Jewish fighter jumps from a window, like a living torch. The Germans stand across the street — and they smile.

Go to the synagogue and say Kaddish!

A picture of Treblinka that must — and will, I hope — drive me mad: Jewish mothers, naked Jewish mothers, lead their children to the *Akedah*. It seems to me that the mothers with the children in their arms go on a carpet of flowers. They go. No. They fly in the air, between heaven and earth, like accursed angels.

So go, take a flower from the field, take a child from a mother and run to say Kaddish!

* * *

The finger turns leaf after leaf, picture after picture, and on the other side of the lake the setting sun immerses itself in its own gold.

The world remains world, men and women have children, peoples prepare themselves for wars, rabbis give sermons, and businessmen make plans, poets sing songs and artists dream of the truth — all as before, all as it once was, as though the entire Holocaust had occurred within a parenthesis of history.

A Jewish leader travels to West Germany and brings the leader of Germany with him to Bergen-Belsen.

Already an American rabbi has nothing else to do than to travel to Germany to give sermons in German schools.

Do they not hear the laughter of the German soldiers? Regimes change, governments come and go — but the murderers' laughter is eternal.

What has happened to our spiritual leaders and guides? How blind and deaf can one be today?

There is a legend that compares the human heart to a well where the dead come to delight themselves with a drink of blood, and the more dear they are to us, the more we love them, the more blood they drink.

So if our great ones are not ashamed to walk over the fields of flowers of Germany, it is evidence that their well has run dry.

* * *

Today is the Yahrzeit of my father's death, and only the eye says Kaddish for him. The tongue would have done so also, except that it is ashamed. "Itchele," (pseudonym of Moshe Bunem Justman, renowned Yiddish journalist and novelist in prewar Warsaw) of blessed memory, it is said, once cried out that the world no longer has possibility, that is, it no longer has the right to exist.

True: if nothing has changed since the Holocaust, if women have not begun having children with three eyes and two heads, if people have not created new religions and new ways, if all has remained the same, then it is a sign that everything is rotten, internally degenerate. The end is in sight.

Immediately after the war — I was still a naive young yeshiva student — I protested against the world that had been silent.

Today I would formulate my cry in another way. Today — the eighteenth day in the month of Shevat — I would accuse myself before all others.

I, too, take pleasure in a good drama. I, too, am in seventh heaven when the Shekhinah, the Divine Presence, rests on my pen. I, too, eat bread and drink wine.

I turn the pages of the Polish picture album, and the murderers, the faces of the hangmen, laugh out to me from several pages. I do not know who they are. I do not know what happened to them.

But I know that Adolf Eichmann lives. I know that Ilse Koch is a happy mother. I know that Dr. Mengele sunbathes in Argentina.

Eichmann was the chief hangman in Hitler's Reich. Hitler entrusted him with the mission of liquidating the Jewish question in Europe. He organized the transports of the Jews from the occupied lands to Auschwitz and Buchenwald.

Ilse Koch was the wife of the commandant of the Buchenwald concentration camp. Every morning she would take a stroll in the *Lager* with her two giant dogs. To entertain herself she would loose the dogs on a prisoner, whom they literally tore to pieces. Ilse Koch had another "hobby." She would make beautiful, colorful lampshades from tattooed skin stripped from prisoners.

Dr. Mengele was the selection commandant in Birkenau. He stood beside the tower and with a rod pointed the way to death or to the death agony.

No Grynszpan or Schwarz-Bart stood up to raise the fist of revenge or the sword of justice against these three mass murderers and their comrades.

Instead of wrestling with the problem of revenge, Jewish boys
went to settle in Germany, where they deal with Germans and carry
on love affairs with their daughters. And if a feeling of shame and
regret awakens in them, American rabbis come and stifle it with
holiday sermons in their synagogues and by taking money for
Jewish causes.

Occasionally they go on Kever Avot to Bergen-Belsen to honor
the dead: they come to the synagogue, say a quick, perfunctory
Kaddish, and are free to think about other matters for a whole year.

God in heaven, you God of vengeance, today's Jew, it appears,
is not created in your image. He does not think of revenge. He
thinks of money and art, about honors and about pushing mankind
a step further. But he distances the dead from his well.

This is why the tongue is ashamed to murmur a Kaddish: the
laughter of a Mengele and an Ilse Koch would deafen it. If the world
is a place of impurity, one must not say Kaddish in it.

Only the eye may say Kaddish. So I walk on the field of flowers
where Jewish mothers lead their children to the Akedah, and out of
shame I want to throw everything away and run like a madman
over lakes and mountains so as not to hear — today, the eighteenth
day in the month of Shevat — the shrill laughter of the demon of
night.

To Bring Hope and Help

by LEO EITINGER

It is generally accepted that being a surgeon is much more impressive than being a psychiatrist.

Just watch an open-heart operation on television: you see the heart beating, the surgeon working — a master over life and death. Then look at the psychiatrist with his patient: they just sit together and talk. Well, anyone can just sit and talk!

Therefore the psychiatrist's prestige is rather low. It follows that a patient very rarely attaches greater importance to treatment by a psychiatrist than by a surgeon. But if it *does* happen, as in the description of Elie Wiesel's operation in Auschwitz in his autobiographical work *Night*, it is a symptom of something quite exceptional. Because what is the essence of a psychiatrist's work? Basically it is trying to be a human being and helping another human being by being humane — in other words, the most natural thing to do in a normal world.

But the world in which Elie Wiesel and I were living was anything but normal, and being — or remaining — a human being was not only strictly forbidden but also extremely dangerous. There were, however, a few people who were privileged to work in surroundings where, to a certain extent, humanity was still allowed and not directly punished. To work as a doctor in the barracks of Auschwitz (these, as a travesty, were called sick bays) was thus a highly appreciated privilege. It was also a very ambivalent and problematic one. To help a sick prisoner back to health meant sending him back to hell. On the other hand, *not* to help him back meant his certain death. And how many of those whom one could send back to work had any chance to survive? No wonder then that one often despaired over the senselessness, the hopelessness of one's work, knowing that the patients died whatever was done.

Incredibly enough, and quite unexpectedly, some survived. How and why? Who can answer these questions here and now?

Previously unpublished, this tribute is printed by permission of the author.

When I started to study survivors nearly 35 years ago, my impressions were as follows:

> Men and women for whom an avenue of beautiful green trees summons up a vision of long rows of gallows with swinging corpses. For them, the sight of an old man is a reminder of the crematoria with thick yellow smoke rising from the chimneys. Peacefully playing children recall other children, emaciated, tortured, murdered. These men and women are burdened with the inescapable memory of columns of grey slaves, beaten and killed when they could no longer keep going, the memory of infirmaries filled with people dying of dysentery, typhus and starvation.
>
> The amount of suffering undergone in the concentration camps of the Second World War defies description: the most gifted writer could not convey to those who have not themselves gone through it the extent and depth of that misery. Only the survivors know and they cannot translate their experience into words and convey it to others.

One tried and succeeded: Elie Wiesel. But even he feels that it is no easy task. And I quote him:

> You will not find it easy to understand them. Indeed, you never did understand them. In spite of appearances, they are not of this world, not of this era. Ask them whether they are happy. No matter what they answer, it will not be true. Ask them whether the future tempts them or frightens them. No matter what they answer, that, too, will not be true.
>
> Ask them whether on the day of their liberation they experienced joy. Permit me to answer in their stead: It is a day I remember as an empty day. Empty of happiness, of feeling, of emotion. Empty of hope. We no longer had the strength even to weep. There were those who recited the Kaddish in an absentminded sort of way, addressing an absent God on behalf of the absent.
>
> We were all absent. The dead and the survivors.

But fortunately, Elie did not remain absent forever. On the contrary, through his books, he has erected a monument to the dead, not of dead stone nor cold marble but of living works of vital importance and burning ideas which will continue to live and to give meaning to the sacrifices and to the memory of the sacrificed victims.

For the survivors he has been a leader and teacher, a beacon in the darkness of our isolation. He has taught us that revenge is not our way to go; that it is the duty of every human being to reduce sufferings, not to enhance them; that it is our most important task to alter sufferings into acts of friendship and generosity. Then, and only then, are they justified.

Elie himself has been the first and foremost to do so, to transform sufferings into tolerance and compassion and to give them a transcendental meaning. He has rebuilt the self-confidence and the human dignity of the survivors and encompassed all the victims of our wretched world with care and love.

And, if I may add a personal note, he has given a new dimension to my life.

Understandably, it was always among the greatest of professional pleasures in my post-concentration-camp life to meet former Auschwitz inmates who said, "You were my doctor," usually exaggerating by continuing, "You saved my life in Auschwitz." In actual fact, one could only alleviate a tiny fraction of our common pain and suffering.

Among the many thousands of patients I saw in the camps, *one* has vindicated our work more than anybody else. Elie has repaid the little given to him by working tirelessly for the cause of humanity, by his unflagging zeal in bringing peace to peoples' minds, by reducing hatred and by offering help to all the persecuted of our time by becoming a sort of psychiatrist of mankind.

In this way he has demonstrated both to the medical community and to the rest of the world the importance and the necessity of bringing hope and help even in the most hopeless and helpless of situations — even on the edge of life and death itself.

TREES

by WILLIAM HEYEN

In the branched galaxy of *Night* when, in Elie Wiesel's words, "the world was a cattle wagon hermetically sealed," Madam Schächter began to cry her vision of the fire to come. Wiesel writes, "Standing in the middle of the wagon, in the pale light from the windows, she looked like a withered tree in a cornfield."

At Birkenau, Wiesel says, "We were so many dried-up trees in the heart of a desert."

Later, Idek the Kapo beats Eliezer's father: "At first my father crouched under the blows, then he broke in two, like a dry tree struck by lightning, and collapsed."

The trees of *Night* wither, they are hermetically sealed, they are dried up, they are struck and split by *SS* lightning. Tree-gallows become black crows in the poignant, helpless, tragic, despairing poetry in the dead heartwood of this deathless book.

On the eve of Rosh Hashanah, "At the place of assembly, surrounded by the electrified barbed wire, thousands of silent Jews gathered, their faces stricken." The wind seemed to speak a benediction: "Blessed be the Name of the Eternal." Wiesel writes, "Thousands of voices repeated the benediction; thousands of men prostrated themselves like trees before a tempest."

Without trees, life on this planet is not possible.

Cut from their roots in the east and buried, felled to freeze into cordwood in deep drifts, reduced to charred remains in the Reich's ovens, the Jews of *Night* are trees. They are, as Wiesel says in *Ani Maamin*, "a forest turned to ashes."

But Wiesel's books are themselves trees. They tremble and almost break in the winds of their experience, but their root systems support them, and him, and us, somehow, somehow.

This previously unpublished essay is printed by permission of Time Being Press, Inc. The poem, "The Tree," originally appeared in *Erika: Poems of the Holocaust.* St. Louis: Time Being Books, 1991. Copyright © 1991 by Timeless Press, Inc.;"The Apple," originally appeared in *Falling from Heaven: Poems of a Jew and a Gentile.* St. Louis: Time Being Books, 1991. Copyright © 1991 by Timeless Press, Inc.

Reading *Night*, when Eliezer is liberated from the camp named "Buchenwald," we wonder what his future will be and think back to words he heard from Moché the Beadle in Sighet: "There are a thousand and one gates leading into the orchard of mystical truth. Every human being has his own gate. We must never make the mistake of wanting to enter the orchard by any gate but our own. To do this is dangerous for the one who enters and also for those who are already there." The gates of Auschwitz and Buchenwald open on/close on/open on "The orchard of mystical truth." From *Night* to *Twilight*, Elie Wiesel, by courage and prayer and devotion and intellect and intuition, would reach this Holocaust orchard where he has been speaking with the barefoot beadle of Sighet, a personage of many guises, ever since. Bless them both.

Reflecting on this theme, I offer the following two poems. This first one is about the life and death and spirit of a village, Lidice.

The Tree

Not everyone can see the tree, its summer cloud of green leaves or its bare radiance under the winter sunlight. Not everyone can see the tree, but it is still there, standing just outside the area that was once a name and a village: Lidice. Not everyone can see the tree, but most people, all those who can follow the forked stick, the divining rod of their heart to the tree's place, can hear it. The tree needs no wind to sound as though wind blows through its leaves. The listener hears voices of children, and of their mothers and fathers. There are moments of great joy, music, dancing, but all the sounds of the life of Lidice: drunks raving their systems, a woman moaning the old song of the toothache, strain of harness on plowhorse, whistle of flail in the golden fields. But under all these sounds is the hum of lamentation, the voices' future. The tree is still there, but when its body fell, it was cut up and dragged away for the shredder. The tree's limbs and trunk were pulped at the papermill. And now there is a book made of this paper. When you find the book, when you turn its leaves, you will hear the villagers' voices. When you hold the leaves of this book to light, you will see the watermarks of their faces.

I like to think that all of us together are reading and writing the book made from that tree, trying to hear those voices, even if this is not possible, trying to see those faces, even if we can see only watermarks.

This next poem began with a few remembered words I heard spoken in the film *Shoah*. It has to do, finally, perhaps, with artistic seeing, with how we must live in order to continue to try to understand. A survivor is speaking. I should say that I always want to remain aware of Mr. Wiesel's words in his essay "A Plea for the Survivors": "Accept the idea that you will never see what they have seen — and go on seeing now, that you will never know the faces that haunt their nights, that you will never hear the cries that rent their sleep. Accept the idea that you will never penetrate the cursed and spellbound universe they carry within themselves with unfailing loyalty."

The Apple

I

In Israel at that time just after the war,
we did not have much to eat,
so when, at the beach, I saw an apple bobbing in the waves,
glistening red, far out, but an apple for sure,
I swam for it.
I did reach the object,
and, as I'd thought, it was an apple.
I carried it to the shore in my bosom,
thinking of its juice and firm flesh.
But, inside, it was rotten:
it had been thrown from a boat,
or a cloud, for good reason.
Were you to eat a bit of my survivor's heart
even the size of an apple seed,
it would poison you.

II

In Israel at that time just after the war,
we did not have much to eat,
so when, at the beach, I saw an apple bobbing in the waves,
glistening red, far out, but an apple for sure,
I swam for it.

I did reach the object,
but it was not an apple.
Unbelievable as this might be, it was an eye,
perhaps from an octopus, or a shark,
or a whale, but an eye,
translucid red, a watery gel,
its pupil black and unmistakable.
Perhaps this was the eye of the angel
of the camps. I cupped it in my hands.
I swallowed at least one mouthful, to see.

NIGHT AS AUTOBIOGRAPHY

by HARRY JAMES CARGAS

Perhaps we can discuss *Night* as autobiography not so much by *comparing* Elie Wiesel's memoir of Auschwitz with other great works in that genre but by *contrasting* it with self-reflections of Augustine, Dante, Rousseau, Wordsworth and others. By making this contrast, we may be able to better grasp the radical break Holocaust autobiography makes from previous expressions of that art form, where similar efforts are found only in the subgenre known as Afro-American autobiography.

Although there is a body of autobiographical literature which pre-dates the *Confessions* of St. Augustine, it is generally agreed that the fifth-century bishop's volume established a base for future essays. Iscorates, Demosthenes and Plato left such pieces as did Cicero, Horace, Ovid, Seneca, Josephus and Marcus Aurelius. But Augustine established the model which became a standard for fifteen centuries, using all three of the forms which autobiography would take up to our own era: historical, philosophical, poetic. These illustrate the three methods of self-knowledge from which those who followed in this genre would select: "historical self-recollection, philosophical self-exploration, and poetic self-expression . . ."[1]

Some will argue that Dante's *La vita nuova* is out of place in this discussion,[2] but I and others disagree. Like Augustine, Dante moves from ignorance to knowledge in his thirteenth-century masterpiece. John Bunyan renders his story in *Grace Abounding*, his own tale of a pilgrim's progress. For Augustine, the truth of his life came in an instant, a moment of conversion; for Dante it came through several revelations, and Bunyan took a lifetime to learn about the meaning of his life.[3]

The *Secretum* is Petrarch's main document for our purposes. He wrote to discover himself, test himself and to clarify himself.[4] Petrarch thus represented where one generally acknowledged the

Previously unpublished, this essay is printed by permission of the author.

need to see the self as distinct from the Church and much of society, where independence and a growing sense of individuality were to be cultivated. This is even more true of the *Life of Benvenuto Cellini*, of which no commentator may ignore Jakob Burckhardt's phrase that he "carries his measure in himself."[5] The French essayist Montaigne, in his *Essais*, goes in a different direction, not, as certain modern existentialist thinkers have urged that he created himself but rather that he attempted to discover the essence of his own being. More like Cellini, Benjamin Franklin presents a life of self-reliance, a kind of how-to book to be used as a guide for living with reference only to this world — an incipient, pragmatic instruction. As one commentator has observed:

> If Augustine's *Confessions* offers an example of the truths revealed in Scripture, and *Grace Abounding* offers a source of divine truth that is as reliable as Scripture, Franklin's *Autobiography* offers itself as Scripture, the only one available to an audience that had overthrown all forms of traditional authority and replaced them with the authority of personal conviction.[6]

Jean-Jacques Rousseau's romanticism offers a new perspective. He cannot suggest specific lessons on how to live because he insists on proving his uniqueness to us. His own *Confessions* are, in part at least, a compilation of his sufferings. He is wiping his brow with a kind of grandiose gesture and asking for our pity. In *The Prelude*, another romantic writer, William Wordsworth, seems more objective in attempting to gain self-knowledge, although that, too, will be found in the interpretation of individual experience.

At about the same time as *The Prelude*, autobiographies of slaves and ex-slaves (often written for them by others) began to appear in this nation. The first is titled *The Interesting Narrative of the Life of Olaudah Equiano, or Gustavus Vassa, the African*, a modest account of terrible experiences. Others include *A Narrative of the Uncommon Sufferings and Surprizing Deliverance of Briton Hamon, a Negro Man* (1760), *Recollections of Slavery* (1838), *Narrative of William W. Brown, a Fugitive Slave* (1847), *The Fugitive Blacksmith; or Events in the Life of James W.C. Pennington* (1849), *The Life of Josiah Henson, Formerly a Slave, Now an Inhabitant of Canada, as Narrated by Himself* (1849), *Twelve Years a Slave; Narrative of Solomon Northrup, a Citizen of New York,*

Kidnapped in Washington City in 1841, and Rescued in 1853, from a Cotton Plantation near the Red River in Louisiana (1853), *Running a Thousand Miles for Freedom: or, The Escape of William and Ellen Craft from Slavery* (1860), and the truly great work, *The Narrative of the Life of Frederick Douglass, an American Slave* (1845).

The tradition of black autobiography continues right up to the present, from Booker T. Washington's still-inspiring *Up from Slavery* and W.E.B. DuBois' five autobiographies (he lived so long he continued to bring them out every decade or so!) to Richard Wright's two volumes, and the contributions of Angela Davis, Eldridge Cleaver (whose *Soul on Fire*, a second work, was enormously disappointing), Claude Brown and so many others. Nor can we overlook the several remarkable reflective books by that genius of letters, Maya Angelou, who can write from pain but who can also celebrate the goodness in all of us.

I am, of course, deliberately ignoring the self-hype autobiographies of contemporary times, those promotional puffs whose only purpose seems to be to justify misspent lives or to convince others that undistinguished lives are somehow made distinguished through some Gutenbergian intervention. These have nothing to do with, if we can go back to oral tradition, the words of the Homeric hero who gives us a true ideal, the *polis*-minded citizen who sees his life as a responsibility, not a "what's-in-it-for-me" venture; or the Roman *pater familias*, Aristotle's man of great mind, the Stoic who bears and accepts what destiny has to offer the dedicated monk, be he Boethius or Thomas á Kempis, who follows the metaphysical ideal, whether it may lead to the stake or to paradisal bliss; or St. Theresa of Avila, the account of whose spiritual journey has been so precious to so many and which gives the lie to the current notion that a mystical experience can be had in minutes, found at the end of a weeded drug.

The ideal knight of the Middle Ages and the country gentleman have each been self-celebrated many times. So have the teacher, the great *magister*, the rabbi whose introspections, as agonizing as some of them were to be made, *were* made for our benefit as well as theirs. As Karl Joachim Weintraub has concluded, these written lives "embody specific life-styles into which to fit the self. They offer man a script for his life . . ."[7]

Let us go back over some of these examples again now and see where Holocaust autobiography in general and Wiesel's memoir

Night, specifically, belong in the scheme labeled "Autobiography." As we do this, there is something to keep in mind: *Night* was originally published in Argentina, in Yiddish, and it was over 800 pages long; the American edition, today, is 109 pages long. When I discussed this with Wiesel in 1972, he told me that he cut away, but to the sensitive reader it is all there.

This cutting away is itself part of a literary tradition — growing more rapidly because of Wiesel's contribution — known as the literature of silence. Here is clearly a style which is most appropriate to the tragedy which is being approached in autobiographies. How does one write about the death of family and friends, of a people, of a culture? One *must,* of course, not permit the murdered to go unremembered. Wiesel, like other Holocaust memoirists, is a messenger for the dead, certain that he cannot say nothing, fearful that what he *does* say might be too much.

This is a matter of sentiment versus sentimentality. Sentiment is a proper emotion, one suited to the dignity of a human being, particularly one in need of comfort, one in pain. Sentimentality is an excess of emotion, something which can be projected by formula and, therefore, which cheapens what ought to be a proper response.

Let me give certain examples from *Night.* When the author and his family arrive in a cattle car at Auschwitz, they are greeted by an SS officer's command: "Men to the left! Women to the right!" Wiesel's stark comment is this: "And I did not know that in that place, at that moment, I was parting from my mother and Tzipora forever."[8]

Another example of understatement, of unwillingness to lapse into sentimentality, occurs when Wiesel witnesses hungry prisoners battling each other for scraps of bread thrown into the cattle cars for the amusement of bystanders. He sees an old man beaten to death by his own son, who wanted the small piece of bread his father had been able to find. Then others beat the son to death. The response: "I was fifteen years old."[9] The reader is left to fill in all of the emotion implied but never rendered on the page.

Finally, there is the scene of the hanging. All of the camp prisoners are forced to witness a twelve-year-old Jewish boy being hanged because he was hungry and sneaked a second cup of the boiled water called soup. (His death was to serve as an example for the rest who experienced that the Kingdom of Night was ruled by the stomach.) The child is so emaciated, however, that it takes him over a half-hour to strangle at the end of his rope. The conclusion is so short, so powerful: "That night the soup tasted like corpses."[10]

Wiesel sees himself following in the steps of other Holocaust writers. In our book of conversations, he tells me about those other authors he admired: "When they began a sentence they could never tell whether they would be alive to finish it: it had to contain everything."[11] He is aware that, often, the less that is said, the more that is communicated with integrity.

Locating *Night* within the framework of autobiography, we must understand Wiesel's idea of language. Here is what he said to me in June of 1988:

> In every word that we pronounce or that we use or that we hear, we must find the ur-word, the original word, the primary word. I would try to find in that word the tone of Adam, when he used the word. When Adam said "I" and I say "I," what is the link between these two "I"s? And this is true of all the other words. If I could read, properly, a word, I could read the history of humankind. This is language, of course, if you trace it, on the highest level of communication and of memory. Language, after all, is a deed of memory. Every word therefore contains not only myself, having said it, but all the people who have said it before me.

This is the seriousness of Wiesel's approach to language.

The paring down of language and the tracing of what the pronoun "I" may fully mean are basic to Elie Wiesel's approach to autobiography.

Like the first autobiographer of distinction, Augustine, Wiesel waited ten years after the major experience of his life to write about it. For the churchman of Hippo, an instantaneous moment of conversion was his impetus. For Wiesel, as we know, it was Auschwitz which was to become his "moment." While Augustine's confession is indeed "an act of total surrender to God, a handing over of oneself, entirely and with utter confidence, into the hands of the only power which could help,"[12] Wiesel's revelation is considerably different. He has no answers; he raises questions.[13]

Augustine's self-questioning, self-discovery and self-evaluation all spring from a confidence in a God of whom the writer is completely certain. The only certainty for Wiesel appears to be that there is no certainty. He writes, "Never shall I forget those flames which consumed my faith forever."[14] He questions God repeatedly, a God who may not be in heaven at all but who may have been hanged on the gallows. Perhaps the only similarity of consequence that we can find between Augustine and Wiesel is that each is a product of his age, and for Wiesel we must add to this recognition an "alas." Each renders the life of a pilgrim, but each is on an entirely different pilgrimage. They are as different as faith and doubt can be. One has been rescued by God; the other may have been abandoned by God.

There is an important similarity which cannot be overlooked. Of Augustine's book, Weintraub has intelligently noted, "In this autobiographic effort the form was created by the personality's need to explain the meaning of life, a need which again and again was to account for the impulse toward autobiography."[15] It would be more accurate — and here is where the distinction is to be emphasized — to say that Wiesel's need was not "to *explain* the meaning of life" but to question it. Where Augustine ends in faith and certainty, Wiesel ends in doubt and perplexity. For Wiesel, the answers change; the questions alone are eternal.

Notable after Augustine is Dante, who, like his searching predecessor, moved from dark to light, advanced from spiritual ignorance to metaphysical knowledge. *Night*, on the other hand, reverses that order, and the protagonist travels from the enlightenment of the midday sun to a darkness so frightening that the only stars he can find in the sky are those he uses for symbols in later works, symbols for dead children's eyes — the million murdered Jewish children, annihilated before they reached their teens.

There is a strong theme of reversals in *Night*. Perhaps the most dramatic of these, as Alvin Rosenfeld has shown,[16] is the reversal of the Abraham-Isaac story, where it is the sons (and there are *several* examples of this in *Night*) who sacrifice their fathers. There is the instance, already alluded to, where the son kills his father to take the bread from him. There is another, in which, on a death march, a son, after having endured misery with his father for years, runs ahead in the march to escape the burden that his father had become. And as *Night* has established the themes of all that Wiesel has written, subsequently, I suggest that this may be the most persistent theme in all of the thirty-six volumes that he has produced to date.

The apologia that the brash and arrogant Peter Abelard wrote in the first third of the twelfth century, titled *Story of My Misfortunes*, and but eighty pages long, was not written as a script to fit a life; rather, Abelard, and his beloved Heloise, it must be added, "strove hard to fit their lives and personalities into scripts already written."[17] In a certain sense, Wiesel's script was somewhat written for him too in terms of an almost totally restricted freedom. However, we remind ourselves, even as Wiesel subtly does in his book, and, as another survivor, psychiatrist Viktor Frankl, insists in his remarkable work of logotherapy, while we may not be free to do very much of our own will, we are totally free to form our attitudes towards whatever restrictions we suffer.

For Petrarch, the Renaissance man was seen to stand alone. But Petrarch and others saw this "aloneness" in a liberating light. Wiesel, too, stands alone, but he has been abandoned. Thus his aloneness is the opposite: an imprisoning darkness, an overwhelming darkness, yet a darkness against which he will courageously struggle and rebel.

If Benvenuto Cellini's autobiography shows us "the person who gives himself the law by which he acts and lives,"[18] Wiesel is desperately searching to see if there in fact is such a law. If Benjamin Franklin's self-presentation is his own scripture, Wiesel recognizes a vacuum. If Montaigne is attempting to discover himself, Wiesel is trying to find out something about God. We cannot help thinking of Montaigne's exclamation: "Man is indeed out of his wits! He cannot create a mite and he creates Gods by the dozen!"[19] Wiesel has powerful words to say, not about the creation of Gods, but of the destruction of human beings, and not dozens of human beings, but millions.

When we consider Rousseau in this context, we cannot be very sympathetic to his appeal to our pity because his soul has been violated. Wiesel has written about people whose souls have been violated, whose bodies have been violated, whose memories have been violated — all deliberately, by plan. But he also has the vision to raise the question of the self-violation of the violators. What impact has the activity of the beastly humans or the human beasts had on the perpetrators themselves? Studies are now appearing in Germany of the consequences of torture on the torturer, in much more detail even than that found in the work of Franz Fanon, who, in colonized Algeria, investigated the effects that torture had on French police officials who abused others purposely. The publications in Germany, by the way, pay particular attention to the damage done to the children and grandchildren of the killers. Recall how Dr. Martin Luther King, Jr., warned us that, in the long run, racism would harm the racists to the greater degree.

Wordsworth, it has been said, wrote his autobiography to gain self-knowledge. Here, again, a contrast with Wiesel is evident. Wiesel seems to write to erase what knowledge he had because it was an error. God did not keep his covenantal agreement with his people; humans did not keep their implied agreement with each other; can there be anything approaching knowledge, certainty, dependability, trust? The query is clearly rhetorical.

There is more of a parallel, and there are more echoes, between black autobiography in America and Wiesel's. The slave narratives, though effusive in their use of language, tell a story of pain and deprivation which is even more concentrated in the volumes of Holocaust autobiography by such survivors as Charlotte Delbo, whose *None of Us Will Return* is a devastating account of murder and dehumanization; Alexander Donat's *The Holocaust Kingdom*, with its anguish of self-doubt; Filip Muller's *Eyewitness Auschwitz*, the horrid, detailed story of atrocities in the crematoria; Primo Levi's *Survival in Auschwitz*, the legacy of which led to the author's suicide more than forty years after liberation; Leon Wells' startling account of *The Death Brigade*; Isabella Leitner's *Fragments of Isabella*, the story of bestiality and its effects; and, of course, in Wiesel's *Night*.

For Augustine, God was the impetus for his autobiography; for Dante, it was his Beatrice; for Bunyan, it was Christ; Ben Franklin's was Reason; Rousseau had his Nature; Wordsworth had poetry; DeQuincy used drug-induced dreams; blacks were, and are, moved through slavery and oppression. For Holocaust authors, of course, the impetus was Auschwitz or the 139 other camps which dotted Europe.

So how are we to react to the reflections of Wiesel and other Holocaust authors' autobiographies? We must offer them gratitude. Each could have easily and understandably concluded that "I have been through enough; I want to forget." Instead, each, like Wiesel, has felt a debt to both the past and the future. Wiesel has written that for him, each word he writes is a tombstone, dedicated to memorializing a death.[20] And he has also told us that he is dedicated to the future as well, dedicated to trying to prevent a holocaust from happening again, to anyone.

NOTES

1. William C. Spengeman, *The Forms of Autobiography* (New Haven: Yale University Press, 1980) 32.

2. Karl Joachim Weintraub, *The Value of the Individual* (Chicago: University of Chicago Press) 62.

3. Spengeman 47-8.

4. Weintraub 98ff.

5. Weintraub 127.

6. Spengeman 54.

7. Weintraub xv.

8. Elie Wiesel, *Night* (New York: Hill and Wang, 1960) 39.

9. Wiesel 103.

10. Wiesel 71.

11. Harry James Cargas, *Harry James Cargas in Conversation with Elie Wiesel* (New York: Paulist Press, 1976) 5.

12. Weintraub 22.

13. Wiesel 16.

14. Wiesel 43.

15. Weintraub 42.

16. Alvin Rosenfeld, *A Double Dying* (Bloomington, Indiana: University Press, 1980) 59.

17. Weintraub 87.

18. Weintraub 121.

19. Weintraub 176.

20. Elie Wiesel, *Legends of Our Time* (New York: Avon, 1970) 26.

THREE POEMS

by ELIE WIESEL

The Oath

Notes from a diary

At the end of their Gathering five thousand survivors pledged an oath at the Western Wall never to forget the Holocaust and never to desecrate it.

Here is the original Yiddish text. The verses in Hebrew, English, French, Russian, and Ladino are not the same.

About the Gathering itself I shall write later. Meanwhile let me simply cite the oath. I composed it on the anniversary of the day the German murderers drove the Jews of my town into the ghetto —

We take the oath in the shadow of candles
That burn like the letters of our alphabet
In the memory of a people:
We swear in the name of parents and children
That never will they be forgotten.

We take this oath with determination,
With hidden sadness and necessary faith:
We swear never to desecrate the sacred memory
Of the holy martyrs
And never to forget.

We saw them in their hunger, in their fear,
In their rush to battle, in the stillness of night:
We saw them on the threshold of the altar.

Silently we grasped their silence
And absorbed their tears in ours:
Tormented mothers rocked dead children —
And smiled.

Ghetto actions, insults, massacres —
Big towns and little, big villages and little,
Young and old, big and small,
They disappeared like clouds afire.

"The Oath" was originally published in *Aler Journal*, June 26, 1981. All three of these poems were translated from the Yiddish by Irving Abrahamson and are printed by permission of the author.

A new Sodom? A fresh flood?
Courageous fighters, pious Jews, young geniuses
And old dreamers of the Messiah,
Clenched fists and torn Books of Psalms:
Do you remember?

The last Seder. The last Sabbath. The last meeting.
The last words of father to daughter.
We swear, here, the oath
In the name of annihilated eternities.

Let it remain as a testament,
A testament from grandfather to son, from son to grandson,
From generation to generation, from vision to word:
Remember what a world, an accursed world,
Has done to our people and to itself.
Remember the martyrs with pride and with sorrow.
Remember the murderer with disgust and rage.

We shall also remember the miracle of revival
And the commandment of fulfillment:
Out of ashes and wounds orphans and widows
Crowned our people Israel with royalty.
Out of ruin we have built old-
New fortresses in the land of our fathers.
To the end of days we will
Remember the heroes, the Jews who have
Elevated the old dream to the highest of heights.

Let us take the oath
Before the holiest in Jerusalem:
Let this testament remain a stone in the Wall,
Because here prayers burn like memories —
They burn and burn and are not consumed.

You Who Are Passing Through

Close your eyes, you who are passing through, and see: a people
almost gone up in flames has taken its graves into heaven
with itself.
Fix your gaze, you who are passing through. Useless his
running. Does he look for gravestones? Useless his
search. There are not enough stones for so many graves.
Only names remain from the thousands and thousands of Jewish
communities: there is nowhere to engrave them.
Nothing to engrave them with.

Bite your lips, you who are passing through, and be quiet: the
enemy has turned the night into a sacrificial altar.
The sacrifices? Jews. All kinds of Jews. Big and small, rich
and poor, pious and free.
Tzaddikim and their fervor, Hasidim and their prayers, beggars
and their alms, young mothers and their lullabies, poor
workers and their tears: the slaughterer slaughtered and
the world was silent.
So, you who are passing through, be quiet also: it is too late
to shout, too late to cry. Your lament will not reach them
by itself.

You want to understand? There is nothing to understand. Too
late, you who are passing through, too late. There is no
longer a road back.
It is a story without a beginning, without an end. No one
will write it. Its secret is the secret of Creation.
Its truth is fearful and eternal, eternal and fearful as the
Lord himself.
You do not want to believe all this really happened? That the
Jew, in the depth of despair, reached the heights? That on
the ruin of hope young lions with clenched fists threw
themselves on the enemy? That nearby witnesses quietly,
without a tear, often with a smile, looked death in the face
and murmured words about *Kiddush Hashem*?
It is good this way, you who are passing through. It is difficult
to believe.

But then, why does the thornbush burn and why is it not consumed?
Do not seek an answer, you who are passing through. Do not
look where you need not. In any case you will not see the fire.
But the inner voice, in the burning bush, do you
hear it? It is their voice.

Tell Me, Good Friends

Good friends,
What are we to do,
What are we to do
When the soul is so burdened?

A generation goes, a generation comes,
The times fly,
Shadows, in haste,
Run away.

We try to remember,
Memory overflows with grief.

Should we try to sing?
Broken is the violin.
The strings torn.

What are we to do,
My good friends,
What are we to do?

Each prayer is
A final outcry,
Each psalm
A quiet Kaddish.

Blind is the sun,
Silent the night.
The dying one is alone,
Far from his grave.

What are we to do,
Good friends,
When the mood
Is so terrifying?

We bite our lips,
We clench our fists,
We say —
What do we say?

Tell me,
My good friends,
Why are you silent?
Where are you?

JEW OF FIDELITY

by EMIL L. FACKENHEIM

It must have been in 1962 or thereabouts that Bob Miller held his annual book sale and offered me Raul Hilberg's *The Destruction of The European Jews* for the low price of five dollars. Bob, a longtime personal friend, was then running the best academic bookstore in Toronto. (He is still at it.) He was, and continues to be, a close friend of mine. Not only that, but my wife, Rose, worked with Bob in his bookstore for years, severing the connection only when, in 1983, we moved to Jerusalem.

Hilberg's book had only just appeared. Few bookstores, I suspect, had acquired any copies. Bob, being Bob, had ordered a copy, but even he just one. And now, less than a year after its appearance, he had put it on sale and offered it to me.

But I declined, saying words to the effect that this particular subject was outside my sphere of interest. In the end I did buy the book anyway, but it was years before I read it from cover to cover.

It could not have been too much later that some of our neighbors walked about gloomily. Ours was a mostly Jewish neighborhood of mostly young couples, a good many with babies who gave the mothers time for reading while they, the babies, were asleep. They were all reading Elie Wiesel's *Night*. Rose read it also but tried to shield me. I cannot remember when I finally did read the book, whether before meeting Elie at a conference in 1965 or after. I rather suspect it was before, for this would explain why, when Rose and I did meet him at a conference, I was predisposed to consider him a person unlike any other — more precisely, *as a Jew* unlike any other.

My earlier "disinterest" in Hilberg's book was no disinterest in things Jewish; these had occupied me since my student days in the 1930s, and I had been publishing essays in what I then called Jewish theology for fifteen years. Nor was it a disinterest in the catastrophes of this century. I had been writing, as the case may have been, philosophically about radical evil in general or theologically about

Previously unpublished, this tribute is printed by permission of the author.

the demonic in general. I had written even about Nazism in particular. But I had avoided the scandalous particularity of the
Holocaust. As a result, I understand all too well now why one does
not have to be either an enemy of Jews or an indifferent Jew in order
to change the subject when the Holocaust comes up, why this can
be done, as it were, even without changing it, such as by diverting
attention from the criminals to the behavior of this or that group of
victims or this or that group of bystanders. I do understand, for I
once did the same thing. In my case, the cause was a hidden fear
that if a Jew faced up to the scandal truly, fully, honestly, the result
would be despair of Judaism. And to find a Judaism that could and
did respond to the catastrophe had been the core of my endeavors
and continues to be so today.

When at last I did read *Night* I was amazed. Here was a book that
did face up to the scandal of Auschwitz truly, fully, honestly. Yet
its every page breathed the conviction that Judaism was not destroyed.
Indeed, paradoxical though it sounds and is, in this book *the innocence of the victims is a cry not only to heaven but also against it; yet
its author's fidelity to that cry is ultimately inspired by the very heaven
at which the cry is directed.* With this book Elie Wiesel emerged as a
Jew of fidelity — to Israel, to the God of Israel, and to the unique
anguish between the two that has come to be ever since the
Holocaust.

Fidelity is the central virtue of a Jew. This was once asserted by
Yehuda Halevi. His *Kuzari* is a dialogue in which a pagan king,
dissatisfied with his paganism, consults, in search of something
better, a philosopher, a Muslim, a Christian and, at length, a rabbi.
In the end he becomes a convert to Judaism. Just prior to that,
however, he has a remaining doubt: he has found greater saintliness and humility among Christians and Muslims. Why, Jews do
not even have monasteries! The rabbi agrees but adds that the
characteristic Jewish virtue is another, namely fidelity. "Consider,"
he says to the king, "how thoughtful men among us could escape
the degradation [of exile] by a word spoken lightly," (i.e., lip-
service conversion to Christianity or Islam). He might have added
that while saintliness is shown by some Christians and Muslims,
fidelity characterizes the Jewish people as a whole, that only
because of it Jews survive at all.

Halevi's observation is out of date, at least in countries in which
Jews need not speak any "words lightly" in order to escape degra-

dation and exile and, indeed, suffer neither. Yet in one respect, if no other, Halevi is more relevant than ever: a Jew's fidelity is insufficient today unless he hears that cry of innocence, a cry that can never be stilled; and this fidelity, like that of his ancestors, has a cost. It risks calumny, such as "narrow parochialism," "traumatization," "victimization by the past" and worse. It also risks loneliness, for who wants to listen to that "ancient history?" (Who wanted to listen when the history was *not* ancient?)

Halevi's Jew of fidelity bore degradation. Today's Jew of fidelity bears calumnies. Better still, he ignores them, knowing in his heart that they are false. This he knows, for even as he hears that cry of Jewish innocence he opens his ears to *every* cry of innocence. As for loneliness, he is not without hope while enduring it. Of this hope Wiesel himself has become a symbol. For if a Jew's fidelity to that cry of Jewish innocence is motivated by fidelity to that very God of Israel at whom it is directed, then it is a testimony not only to Jews alone but to all humanity and in behalf of Him who is both the God of Israel and the Creator of the world.

That Wiesel's fidelity has not weakened over the years is proven by his public criticism of the current occupant of Peter's throne. In 1987, the Vatican beatified Edith Stein as if this Christian nun had risked death for her faith, when in fact she was murdered for her Jewish birth. A year later the Pope himself went even further. Having visited Mauthausen, he declared that "Christians, Jews and others" had given a gift to humanity by their suffering. Whether intentionally or inadvertently, so Wiesel charged publicly, this was tantamount to "de-Judaizing" the Holocaust.

The suffering of "Christians and others" at Mauthausen may be viewed as a gift to humanity, for it was due to their deeds (i.e., acts of opposing Nazism); thus it falls into the category of martyrdom, time-honored within Judaism and Christianity alike. But Jews? They suffered what they did on account not of deeds but of birth. To understand their choiceless death as a "gift" to humanity is humanly impossible.

Can the humanly impossible be made divinely possible? Can the Jewish catastrophe be transsubstantiated into a Christian triumph? The Holocaust was not only a Jewish but also a Christian catastrophe, and for Christians to evade it is to court spiritual disaster.

This is why Wiesel could not be silent. His Jewish fidelity would have failed had he not protested that the Holocaust may be de-

Judaized by Christians no more than by Jews. Wiesel's protest was an act of Jewish fidelity to Jews, to Christians and to the God of both.

ELIE WIESEL: A LASTING IMPRESSION

by PAUL BRAUNSTEIN

When I first met Elie, I did most of the talking. He was semicomatose for most of four or five days, and he didn't talk back much during that period. He slowly recovered, and I remember my first impressions of this man. I didn't know him. He was brought in through an ambulance service. He was a frail little thing, and when he began to talk . . . first of all, he was a very lonely person. I saw no family. I saw no friends visiting him, and, as I talked to him and he became more rational and could get away from the terrible torment he was undergoing because of his injuries, I realized this was a very troubled man. He seemed to be — besides being racked with pain — racked with doubts about man and doubts about his God. I spent many, many hours with him. I was able to do this — I don't think very many people ever get a chance to spend many hours with Elie, but I did — because he was in a big body cast, and he couldn't walk away from me! Well, those were probably some of the most rewarding hours I've ever spent in my life. It became obvious. I came home to my wife after the first several days and said, "Barb, this guy's a real zinger!" And he was. He was profound. It was obvious that this man was destined for great things.

I often missed my fatherly duties at home, and, with a large family, that means administering discipline to your children after their misdeeds of the day; but our family survived it.   Elie's description of the camps and his life in the camp made an impression on me that I will take to my deathbed. I had obviously read about it in the news — horrible things after the war. It made a lasting impression on me, but it was a very superficial impression compared to what I gathered and stored from my long talks with Elie.

I think we became very fast friends. Surgeons don't like to become friends with their patients because it clouds their decision making when they have an emotion put into a rather materialistic

Previously unpublished, this tribute is printed by permission of the author.

decision on what to cut and what not to cut. But I think in my lifetime that Elie has been one of those exceptions.

Really, I have one other point I'd like to make. Harry Cargas has described me in one of his works as the man who saved Elie's life. I didn't save his life. A whole bunch of people saved his life. There were many dedicated young people — nurses, therapists. I was just one cog in a big wheel. And, in retrospect, I don't think we could have lost Elie despite his terrible injuries because I believe in the wisdom of God. I truthfully believe that God had to have Elie to be the conscience of man about the Holocaust and about genocide.

ELIE WIESEL'S
SECOND-GENERATION WITNESS:
PASSING THE TORCH OF REMEMBRANCE

by ALAN L. BERGER

Responding to an interviewer, Elie Wiesel defines the task of a witness in a manner which transcends spatial and temporal constraints. The Nobel Peace Prize winner observes that, "A witness is a link. A link between the event and the other person who has not participated in it. A witness is a link between past and present, between man and Man, and man and God."[1] But what does it mean to be a second-generation witness *after* the Holocaust? How can the second, and successive, generation(s) bear witness to an event they have not personally encountered? Moreover, exactly what are they bearing witness to? One of the most dramatic events in Wiesel's writing is his increasing focus on the second-generation witness. This focus underscores Wiesel's belief that bearing witness is an act of salvific import and coincides both with increased societal awareness of the *Shoah* and, more recently, the appearance of novels written by sons and daughters of Holocaust survivors.[2]

Wiesel's second-generation witness is a complex phenomenon. The nameless horror of extermination camps and the multiple degradations inflicted upon the Jews belong to the survivors' memory. Yet the cultural, psychic, and theological legacy of the disaster is manifest in the lives of their children. For example, Ariel, the protagonist in Wiesel's *The Fifth Son*, observes, "I suffer from an Event I have not even experienced."[3] Consequently, there is a *paradigm shift* in the manner of imaging the Holocaust. Holocaust images among Wiesel's second-generation witnesses reflect their *own* memories: observing their parents' continuing survival, hearing tales or listening to silences, wondering about their role in the family, lighting Yahrzeit candles, obsessional reading about the

Previously unpublished, this essay is printed by permission of the author.

Shoah, pilgrimages to European communities long-purged of their Jewish inhabitants, and a strong identification with the State of Israel. All of these actions emphasize Wiesel's central contention: listening to a witness makes a listener a witness.[4] Consequently, there is a commitment to transmit parents' tales, which become part of the offspring's legacy.

But this is to jump ahead of the discussion. First it is necessary to identify the characteristics of Wiesel's paradigm of the second-generation witness. In so doing, I note both his growing concern with this phenomenon as well as a change in the role of witness. For example, while once he wondered if even those who were in the death camps could ever truly reveal the evil they experienced, Wiesel now sees the second generation as a vital link in the chain of transmitting the tale of the Holocaust. In an interview, he emphasizes that

> The second generation is the most meaningful aspect of our work. Their role in a way is even more difficult than ours. They are responsible for a world they didn't create. They who did not go through the experience must transmit it.[5]

I want to trace the stages of Wiesel's notion of the second-generation witness while noting the development of a dialectic between memory and imagination. This relationship assumes its rightful place alongside the earlier and continuing tension between speech and silence which characterizes Wiesel's *oeuvre*. For Wiesel, imagination must never assume the role of memory. Moreover, imagination requires that an individual be sensitive to history and recognize his/her own role in transmitting the Jewish tale. Much in the Hasidic manner which infuses his life and works, Wiesel believes that tales have the power to transform their listeners. I will conclude by examining how Wiesel's model helps contribute toward further understanding of how both Jewish identity and the post-Auschwitz covenant are expressed in the second-generation witness.

THE WIESELIAN MODEL

Wiesel's second-generation witness is concerned with identity and pedagogy, or, rather, the identity of this generation is itself a type of pedagogical attempt to instruct the world about the horrors of genocide. This attempt involves interrogation of God and man. Traditional teachings are examined in light of catastrophic upheaval. The purpose of this interrogation is to respond to the question asked by Malkiel ("God is my king"), a second-generation witness in Wiesel's *The Forgotten*: "How do we stay Jewish in a world that rejects Jews?" (87). Moreover, Wiesel's second-generation witnesses provide a distinctive angle of vision on the nature and viability of the post-Auschwitz covenant — a point to which I will return later. The urgency of the second-generation witness can be posed in two questions. What does it mean to be a Jew after Auschwitz? Are there universal lessons to be learned from the Jewish catastrophe?

Wiesel links Jewish identity to the act of testimony. "To be a Jew today," he writes, ". . . means: to testify." This testimony bears witness "to what is, and to what is no longer," and takes one of two directions. For example, he asserts that "One can testify with joy — a true and fervent joy, though tainted with sadness — by aiding Israel. Or with anger-restrained, harnessed anger, free of sterile bitterness — by raking over the ashes of the Holocaust."[6]

Consequently, witnessing to the Holocaust is a fundamental ritual of Jewish identity. Moreover, the act of testimony serves to define an historical era. For example, Wiesel observes that each age produces a distinctive type of literature. "If," he writes, "the Greeks invented tragedy, the Romans the epistle, and the Renaissance the sonnet, our generation invented a new literature, that of testimony."[7] So, to testify means both to bear witness to the Jewish experience and to comment on the phenomenon of state-sponsored, systematic annihilation which characterizes and scars the twentieth century.

Wiesel's notion of the second-generation witness evolves out of his long line of literary characters, who, as Ellen Fine argues, are themselves "the witnesses of the witness."[8] These witnesses, in turn, provide "insights for both the reader and the author."[9] For Wiesel, the survivor witness has a three-fold obligation: he/she must remember, testify, and transmit.[10] But how does he understand the role of the second-generation Holocaust witness? Addressing the First International Conference of Children of Holocaust Survivors, Wiesel articulates the relationship between the witnessing of survivors and that of their children. He states that survivors "have shown what they can do with their suffering; you are showing what you can do with your *observation of their suffering.*" [emphasis added][11] But suffering is not an end in itself. If one invokes suffering, it should be to "limit suffering."[12] Moving beyond the narrow confines of clinical studies which reduce children of survivors to pathology, Wiesel notes that many in the second generation have "rechanneled [their] sadness, . . . anger, [and] inherited memories into such humanistic endeavors as medicine, law, social action, education, philanthropy."[13] But more than humanistic endeavors are involved. Wiesel endows the second-generation witness with a mission "to keep the [survivors'] tale alive — and sacred."[14]

THE SECOND-GENERATION WITNESS IN WIESEL'S NOVELS

Wiesel's elevation of the second-generation witness is an evolving concept which occurs over a period of time spanning nearly two decades and reflects an emphasis on hope in the author's ceaseless theological dialectic between hope and despair. From *The Oath* (1973), through *The Testament* (1981) to *The Fifth Son* (1985) and, most recently, *The Forgotten* (1992), he provides increasing detail about the identity, mission, and role of this witness. For example, *The Oath* depicts an anonymous son of survivors. Confused and marginalized, the youth's present and future are jeopardized by his mother's Holocaust past. The young man contemplates suicide. About this figure, Wiesel observes, "He arouses our pity because he doesn't even have the consolation of being a witness. He represents all my students and all the young people who are so perplexed today."[15]

Pity is, however, only the first stage. The youth's search for meaning transforms into a mission. His life is saved by Azriel ("whom God helps"), the novel's narrator and sole survivor of a pre-Holocaust conflagration of Jews in the village of Kolvillag ("every village," or "the entire world"). Azriel is the keeper of his father Shmuel's *pinkas* (communal archive). Long ago, he took an oath of silence, vowing never to reveal the village's horrible fate. Kolvillag suffered a murderous pogrom after the Jews were falsely accused of murdering a Christian child. Moché, thinking that he could save his fellow Jews by confession to the "crime" (the child was not murdered), argues for silence. The Jews, he contends, "have been mankind's memory and heart too long. Too long have we been other nations' laughingstock. Our stories have either amused or annoyed them. Now we shall adopt a new way: silence" (243). In Moché's view, the world does not deserve to hear Jewish testimony. Shmuel ("God hears") adopts a different position. He insists on memory and the necessity to testify. In this manner, Wiesel presents his own struggle with the dialectic between the imperative of speech and the desire to embrace silence.

Years later, Azriel breaks his vow in order to save the young man's life. He tells the youth that he now has no right to die. Henceforth his mission will be to tell Azriel's tale. Consequently, bearing witness can be salvific. Azriel's act of testimony both saves the young man's life and compels the youth, in turn, to tell the story. Azriel emphasizes this in declaring to the young man, "Because now, having received this story, you no longer have the right to die" (286). In Fine's words, "this child of survivors is the listener who, in turn, becomes the narrator — the person responsible for transmitting the book. He is . . . the inheritor of the testimony."[16]

At this point, the second-generation witness is depicted metaphorically. Lacking a clear personality of his own, he is a second "only" child of a mother obsessed with the death of her first family. The mother suffers from nightmares and melancholy, constantly rebuking herself for failing to accompany her five-year-old son after his selection for death. Unable to communicate with his mother, the youth is overwhelmed by the Holocaust's continuing devastation and wonders, "Where do I fit in? I suffered with her and for her, but I could not understand" (67). At this stage of his writing, Wiesel observes of the second-generation witness, "Born after the Holocaust, you have inherited the burden but not the mystery. And you were told: Go ahead, do something with it." But what can one do with such a legacy? Wiesel calls it a "*treacherous situation*" (65, emphasis added). One can neither disregard the Holocaust nor continue without disregarding it. The problems are both theological and secular. Characteristically, Wiesel expresses them as questions: ". . . how is one to worship a heaven splattered with mud?"; "What is the good of prolonging a civilization wallowing in ashes?" (64). The dilemma of the Holocaust is fundamental. "Dealing with it," writes Wiesel, "poses as many problems as turning away" (65).

Yet *The Oath* contains the seeds of hope which will later sprout in the other three novels. The novel in fact marks a turning point in Wiesel's writing where, for the first time, life triumphs over despair. The novel's message, attests Michael Berenbaum, "involves a positive affirmation of life which moves beyond despair. Wiesel has moved from a protest against death to an outright appeal to life. . . . For the first time in any of Wiesel's novels, the major narrator clearly advocates life."[17] For example, the mission to bear witness saves the young man's life. Silence is never justified in the presence of a life-threatening situation. Moreover, by linking Azriel's testimony of a pre-*Shoah* destruction of Jewish life to the catastrophe of the Holocaust symbolized by the son of survivors, Wiesel underscores the historical seamlessness of Jewish identity and its imperative to bear witness.

The Testament, which appeared almost a decade after *The Oath*, pursues the theme of the second-generation witness through the prism of a father's testament to his son. The novel opens in Israel but encompasses a half-century of Jewish history in Russia while detailing Paltiel Kossover's peripatetic life and martyrdom. Paltiel, whose name means both "God is my refuge" and "I am a refugee from God," is a poet imprisoned by Stalin. Wiesel confides that he is a composite figure based on the poet Peretz Markish and the novelist Der Nister, two of the Jewish writers murdered by Stalin's order.[18] Awaiting execution, Paltiel writes his testament for his young son, Grisha. The father, who began as a religious Jew, relates the tale of his rebellion against Judaism and his subsequent embrace of Communism. His journeys have taken him throughout Europe. He has lived in Berlin and Paris and participated in the Spanish Civil War. His comrades also sent Paltiel on a mission to Palestine. Rejecting his earlier infatuation with Communism, which he now terms "Godless messianism," [19] he reembraces his Jewish identity. His testament is an account of Jewish suffering, a rejection of communist illusions, and a mature embrace of *Ahavat Israel* (love of the Jewish people). Wiesel in fact terms this novel a story of repentance. "Written in prison," he observes, "this testament frees others from prison."[20] Implicit in this remark is that the prison to which he refers is the illusion of any redemptive system which refuses dignity to individual human beings.

Grisha, a nickname for Gershon (the Gershonites were associated with both the Tabernacle and, later, the Jerusalem Temple), for his part, is mute. His grandparents were murdered in the *Shoah*. At age two, he last saw his father, and five years later bit his own tongue in two in order to keep from betraying the imprisoned man. Estranged from his mother, the boy is befriended by Viktor Zupanev, a night watchman and former stenographer in the prison where Paltiel was murdered. Zupanev smuggles Paltiel's manuscript out of the prison and gives it to Grisha who, in turn, bears his father's testament to Jerusalem. The watchman assumes the role of father-teacher of Grisha while observing an important fact for the notion of the second-generation witness. "Each generation," attests the watchman, "shapes its own truth" (108). Answering his own question about who will tell the truth when the witnesses to that truth have been murdered, Zupanev tells Grisha, "Yes, my boy, the mute poets will cry forth our truth. Are you ready?" (108).

Grisha's muteness is the novel's key element and can be seen on a variety of levels. For example, Fine intelligently argues that the constant tension in Wiesel's work between speech and silence is "resolved through the creation of a fictional character — a child of the second generation — who cannot speak and thus, need not struggle against himself."[21] In the context of Wiesel's evolving portrayal of the second-generation witness, however, it is equally plausible to assume that the muteness is meant to stand for the difference between the first- and second-generation witnesses. The second generation wants to bear witness but is, in this case, literally unable to speak.[22] Yet Grisha first memorizes and then transcribes his father's Testament, thus assuming responsibility for disseminating its message of the meaning of Jewish identity. Before leaving Russia, Zupanev tells Grisha, "in turn you will assume your role: you will speak on behalf of your dead father" (38). Transmitting his father's memory in Israel, Grisha adds to it his own while observing that "my father is a book and books do not die" (39). Jewish memory will continue. At this stage, Wiesel's second-generation witness begins to assume an increased measure of Jewish identity and responsibility for maintaining the tradition.

With the appearance of *The Fifth Son* and *The Forgotten*, Wiesel specifically focuses on the second-generation Holocaust witness. Each of the novels is set primarily in America, thus emphasizing his conviction that the *Shoah* is a concern of all Jews; both novels tell their story through a father-son relationship; and each charges the second-generation witness with the task of preserving and transmitting survivor memory while, simultaneously, acknowledging the difference between survivors and their offspring. The imagination of the second generation must not be substituted for the knowledge of the survivors. Nevertheless, both novels individualize the second generation while revealing a range of emotions towards their survivor parents and emphasizing an embrace of Jewish identity which is inextricably connected to the *Shoah*.

Wiesel dedicates *The Fifth Son* to his own son, Elisha, and, through him, to all children of survivors. The novel, in fact, marks a *sea change in Wiesel's writings*.[23] For the first time, he changes his voice from that of a survivor to a child of survivors in attempting to portray the intergenerational tensions and traumas in survivor families. Wiesel captures the second generation's plight in experiencing the effects of the *presence of an absence*. For example, Ariel, whose name means "lion" or "Mountain of God" but may also refer to the destruction of Jerusalem, observes that "the children of survivors are almost as traumatized as the survivors themselves." "From a past that made history tremble," the boy continues, "I have retained only words" (192). Like *The Oath*'s nameless second-generation witness, Ariel is confused about his role within the family. Reflecting the impact of his Holocaust inheritance, he wonders, "What am I to do with a life that is not mine?" (166).

His family is psychically ruined by the *Shoah*. The boy's father, Reuven, preoccupied with the past, conceals his memories from Ariel. Reuven (see, a son) writes letters to his first son, also named Ariel, who was murdered by the Nazis. The father questions and undermines the traditional Jewish covenant by asking, "Is it true that God always intervenes? Did he save our generation? He saved me. Is that reason enough for me to tell Him of my gratitude?" (42). About his mother, Rachel, Ariel says, "[she] looks at me but doesn't see me" (39). She is institutionalized and dies near the novel's conclusion. Like *The Oath*'s survivor mother, both parents are tormented by the memory of their murdered son.

Similar to the anonymous second-generation figure in *The Oath*, Ariel is a second "only" son. Unlike his fictional predecessor, however, he is a professor at a small Eastern university who teaches his students the story of the Holocaust and its aftermath in hopes that knowledge of the Event will compel action to prevent new geno-

cidal acts. Consequently, the second-generation witness here assumes a pedagogical task within a secular context which nonetheless
has salvific potential. Before he teaches others, however, he himself
must first learn. He accomplishes this mission in several ways.
Initially, he listens to tales of the *Shoah* which are told by his father's
friend Bontchek. It is from this survivor that he learns the fate of the
Jews in the ghetto of Davarowsk. Ariel also devours books about
the Holocaust. Following his father's example, the American-born
Ariel begins composing letters to his murdered namesake, thereby
assuming a personal relationship to the Holocaust past. Finally, he
travels to Reshastadt ("evil city") in Germany, in order to confront
Richard Lander, the Nazi "Angel of Death," now a successful
businessman, who had liquidated the Davarowsk ghetto and
murdered the first Ariel. Dismissing both vengeance and inherited
guilt, Ariel returns to America confirmed in his mission to bear
witness.

Through contextual reference both to the Passover Haggadah
and the Holocaust, Wiesel links a foundational salvific event of
Jewish history and the twentieth-century event whose aim it was to
destroy that history. The Haggadah (from the verb *l'haggid*, "to tell")
speaks of four sons to whom the tale of the Exodus must be related.
These sons emblemize attitudes towards Jewish history. The wise
son displays wisdom and interest in his detailed questions concerning
the Exodus. The wicked son excludes himself from the Passover
ritual and, consequently, denies the covenant by asking, "What
does this service mean to you?" "To you" (he says) — but not to
him.[24] The simple son, for his part, is sincere but ignorant. The
fourth son is one who is insufficiently mature to enquire.

These attitudes reflect society's understanding of the Holocaust
as well as represent stages through which an individual may pass.
For example, Rueven tells Ariel that prior to the Holocaust he had
abandoned his own Jewish identity in favor of secular culture and
thereby came to represent the wicked son. Reuven only came to
study Judaism in Davorowsk when, as Nazi-appointed leader of
the ghetto's Jews, he was tutored by Rabbi Aharon Asher. The holy
man's instructions were simple: "I am not asking you to practice
your religion, only to know it" (99). The rabbi is subsequently
martyred. Abandonment of Judaism is, for Wiesel, a refusal to bear
witness and, thus, a threat both to Jewish continuity and to human
survival. (For example, turning one's back on Judaism is also

displayed by *The Oath*'s Azriel when, shortly after his bar mitzvah, he temporarily embraces Communism, and also by Paltiel Kossover in *The Testament*.) After Auschwitz, which represents the *anti-Exodus par excellence*, the Passover Seder refers to a fifth son. He is the absent one murdered in the Holocaust. The presence of this absence forms the core of *The Fifth Son*'s attempt to portray the profound effect of survivor melancholy and sadness on the second generation. The Seder symbolism is also highly suggestive in personalizing the Jewish peoples' response to history. "In every generation," states the Haggadah, "one is obliged to see himself as though he himself had actually gone forth from Egypt." Consequently, *The Fifth Son* contends that all Jews are bound eternally both to the Exodus and to the memory of the *Shoah*.

Ariel struggles to achieve his own identity while simultaneously feeling "crushed by the weight of the past" (165). He confides that his life is one of restraint: "What I wish to say, I shall never say. What I wish to understand, I shall never understand" (219). The experience of the Holocaust both defines and eludes him. Different from both the survivors and his American peers, Ariel wonders if he can ever live his own life. Unlike *The Testament*'s Grisha, Ariel can speak, yet he knows that his words fall short of the mark. This is part of the burden of the second-generation witness. Nevertheless, telling the tale is Ariel's way of continuing the story which binds the generations, incorporating the *Shoah* into Jewish collective memory.

At this point in his writing, Wiesel adds a *new dimension* to his dialectic between the desire for silence and the compulsion to testify. The second-generation witness, as noted earlier, emphasizes the tension between memory and imagination. For example, Bontchek tells Ariel Holocaust tales which "fuel" his imagination. Consequently, while the second generation does not have direct experience of the *Shoah*, its members have an intensely personal relationship to the Holocaust. For example, Ariel observes that "War, for me, is my mother's closed face. War, for me, is my father's weariness" (192-193). Yet, imagination, attests Wiesel, is damaging when it assumes the authority of knowledge.[25] Therefore, if the second-generation witness is to fulfill the Wieselian task of keeping "the tale alive and sacred," members of this generation must speak neither instead of nor for the survivors; rather, the second-generation witness is one who attests to the ongoing effects of the *Shoah* both in the lives of the survivors and their offspring.

In *The Forgotten* Wiesel places unprecedented emphasis on the second generation's witnessing task even while reaffirming the difference between survivors and their children.[26] Elhanan Rosenbaum is a survivor and a psychotherapist. A widower, he lives in New York with his son, Malkiel. The father, a victim of Alzheimer's disease, must transmit his Holocaust story to Malkiel before his memory is completely destroyed. To remember is in fact a sacred task. Wiesel emphasizes this linkage by having Elhanan pray to God, who is the Lord of both Sinai and Auschwitz. The survivor implores God to help him, because to "forget is to repudiate" (11). Elhanan poses a question to God which underscores the privileged status of survivor testimony: "What sort of witness would I be," queries Elhanan, "without my memory?" (12). By describing a survivor whose memory is failing, Wiesel underscores the fact that while survivor stories will never fully be known, it is necessary to preserve the fragments that we have. The novel portrays how the second generation inherits survivor memory while reemphasizing that this memory is ineffable. Witness of the witness, Malkiel listens to and records Elhanan's memories. Unlike Reuven in *The Fifth Son*, who intentionally refrains from speaking about the Holocaust to his son, Elhanan does little else but share his memories with Malkiel.

One major difference between *The Fifth Son* and *The Forgotten* is dialogical. In the former novel, Ariel reports his father's sense of melancholy and remorse (Reuven mistakenly thought that his postwar attempt to assassinate Lander had succeeded); Reuven is "off in a distant universe" (48), he "was afraid of children; they frightened him and brought back his old fear. And so did I" (21). Ariel's images of his father include holiness, anger, separation, impotence, and, above all, silence. On the other hand, *The Forgotten* portrays a multilayered relationship, one in which the survivor and his son speak on topics ranging from politics, to love, to God. Malkiel, who is a journalist, spends Sabbaths and holy days with Elhanan and visits him as often as possible at other times. Indeed, their mutual caring and concern is reminiscent of the father-son relationship in Wiesel's classic memoir *Night*. In both *Night* and in *The Forgotten*, the son's task is to continue the father's story.

Malkiel learns a crucial second-generation lesson. Rebelling as a teenager, he is reminded by Elhanan that the young man's refusal to bear witness is a repudiation of the survivor's life. Traveling to his father's natal village of Feherfalu ("white village"), in Romania, in order to know him better, Malkiel meets figures from the Holocaust past. Hershel the gravedigger tells the young man an extraordinary tale about the Great Reunion, a time when souls of saintly rabbis convened a *Bet din* (Rabbinic court) in the village cemetery to decide how to help Feherfalu's persecuted Jews. Malkiel also learns that Hershel assassinated the head of the anti-Semitic Nyilas. One of Malkiel's most striking encounters is with Ephraim, a blind survivor and Elijah-like figure who embodies memory itself. Ephraim tells Malkiel about the heroism of the young man's grandfather, who was martyred by the Nazis for protecting his fellow Jews. In a dramatic scene, Ephraim symbolically transmits the torch of remembrance to Malkiel. "The blind man," writes Wiesel, "leaned toward Malkiel as if to inspect him; their heads touched. The old man's breath entered Malkiel's nostrils" (196). This literal transferral of survivor memory is Wiesel's clearest statement to date on the importance he assigns the second-generation witness.

This is, however, as previously noted, a dialectical relationship between survivors and second-generation witnesses which both allows for transmitting memories of the *Shoah* and limits its possibilities. On the one hand, Malkiel echoes the action of *The Testament*'s Grisha. Visiting his grandfather's grave, Malkiel vows to bear witness in his father's place. The second-generation witness states, "I will speak for him. It is the son's duty not to let his father die" (232). Unlike Grisha, however, Malkiel transmits not his father's book but paternal stories and the tales of other survivors as well. Elhanan attempts literally to transfuse his memory to Malkiel. "In proportion as Elhanan felt his memory diminish," writes Wiesel, "Malkiel felt his own expand" (177). Yet for the second-generation witness, the presence of an absent memory is itself twice-filtered, once by what the survivor reveals and secondly by the ineluctable nature of the Event itself. For example, Malkiel, in his father's Carpathian village, articulates the dialectic between survivors and the second-generation witness. On the one hand, recognizing that the second generation needs to find its own voice and way to remember, Wiesel has the son observe of his relationship to his father's Holocaust experience, "I can live after you and even for you, *but not as you*" (147, emphasis added). Malkiel understands that Elhanan has made him his messenger and that he "will have to

prove [himself] worthy of the message." Yet, even while recognizing the need for the second-generation witness, Wiesel privileges
survivor testimony by having Malkiel say, "I know that whoever
listens to a witness becomes one in turn; you told me that more
than once. But we are not witnessing the same events. All I can say
is, I have heard the witness" (148).

Several dimensions of Wiesel's second-generation witness emerge
from this discussion. Survivor testimony is sacrosanct. Deprived
of this status, the second generation must resort to imagination.
But imagination alone is itself problematic and invites trivialization.
Consequently, Wiesel seeks to ground second-generation imagination in history. He outlines three paths for this witness: listen to
survivor testimony, make pilgrimages to the destroyed Jewish
communities of Europe, and do not allow imagination to replace
survivor memory. Moreover, the universal nature of the second-
generation testimony emerges from its Jewish specificity. Characteristically, Wiesel expresses the relationship between particular
and universal in aphoristic form. He writes, ". . . we must
remember the six million Jews and, *through them and beyond them
but not without them*, rescue from oblivion all the men, women and
children who perished in those years in the camps and forests of
the kingdom of night." [emphasis added][27] Consequently, the
message of authentic second-generation witnesses speaks to all of
humanity. Finally, bearing witness entails taking personal responsibility for speaking about the Holocaust.

WIESEL'S ADDITIONAL COVENANT

Wiesel's tales and stories, and his notion of the second-generation
witness, attest to a new covenantal model. Convinced that the
covenant was broken at Auschwitz, he believes that the conventional God is no longer an answer but rather a question.[28] Nevertheless, Wiesel remains steadfastly Jewish, and his work constitutes
an extensive *din Torah*, or trial of God. Wiesel's deity is still the
Riboyne Shel O'lem (Master of the Universe), but He is no longer
either just or merciful. Moreover, echoing the kabbalistic notion of
a God in need of salvation and the Hasidic belief that the road to
God leads through man, Wiesel's writings suggest the outlines of
a new covenant. The God of this covenant is a diminished deity
whose existence depends on the affirmation of the Jewish people.[29]

Wiesel's post-Auschwitz understanding of the relationship between God and the Jewish people has been termed an "additional
covenant," which "can no longer be between humanity and God or
Israel and God, but rather between Israel and its memories of pain
and death, God and meaning."[30]

This additional covenant emphasizes that Jewish identity is
based on memory and one's own choice to remain Jewish. Those
who give testimony after Auschwitz attest to the solidarity of the
Jewish people, express a commitment to witness to the sheer
endurance of Jewish survival, and affirm their belief in the sanc-
tification of life. The additional covenant, while acknowledging
the diminishment of God and the reality of evil, refuses despair.
Rather, the tales and stories told by survivors and the second-
generation witnesses exemplify the Messianism of the unredeemed.[31]
This Messianism has an individual rather than a cosmic focus and
represents Wiesel's determination to attest to the shattering impact
of Auschwitz while affirming his commitment to Jewish teachings
about Messiah, although this Messiah is symbolized by human
rather than divine acts.[32]

CONCLUSION

Wiesel's second-generation witnesses open a dialogue with the
past in order to inform the present and help chart a course for the
future. These witnesses are committed to testify about the *Shoah*
and thereby take responsibility for attempting to improve a world
in which genocidal ways of thinking remain prevalent. Unlike their
creator, these literary second-generation witnesses are driven less
by theology and more by psychology and sociology, or, rather,
their psychosocial concerns are fraught with theological signifi-
cance. Wiesel's use of theonomous names reveals his belief that the
witness is performing a sacred act. The Jewish identity of Wiesel's
second generation is formed by their "witnessing of the witnesses."
Questions about God and history, absent siblings and vanished
relatives are woven into a post-Auschwitz midrash which seeks to
confront the murder of the Jewish people by incorporating their
memory into the fabric of Jewish continuity.

The strongly autobiographical emphasis of the second generation is a hallmark of modern reflection on the meaning of Jewish
identity. Clearly it is not restricted to the second-generation witness.

Anyone who honestly opens her/himself to encountering the terrible evidence of the *Shoah* finds that the awesome events enter into and transform their very being. Consequently, the serious investigator is compelled to reexamine all aspects of her/his life even though, as Wiesel writes, they "will view the agony and death of a people from afar, through the screen of a memory that is not [their] own."[33] Nevertheless, Wiesel's second-generation witness bears a special obligation to speak on behalf, but never *instead*, of the survivors. This is a crucial distinction in facing the question of how the *Shoah* will be remembered a century from now.

Not all of Wiesel's literary second-generation witnesses share either his knowledge of or commitment to traditional Jewish religious thought and behavior.[34] These witnesses begin as passive recipients of survivor testimony whose allegiance to Judaism is vague and inchoate (*The Oath*). The second-generation witness then, like Abraham of antiquity, abandons a land of idolatry and travels to Israel, the only place he can achieve authentic Jewish identity while transmitting his father's book (*The Testament*). Wiesel then turns to the complexity of survivor families in *The Fifth Son* and *The Forgotten*. The former stresses the catastrophe's psychic legacy while tracing the steps taken by the second-generation witness to learn his family history in order to embrace his Jewish destiny. On the other hand, Wiesel's most recent second-generation witness presents the reader with a different dimension of both survival and witnessing. Intimately involved with the history of his people, Elhanan transmits both his love and desperation to Malkiel, who, in turn, is actively involved in discovering all he can about Judaism and the *Shoah* so that he may bear informed witness. Unlike Ariel, whose concerns were primarily psychological, Malkiel reveals a deepened understanding of the theological dimensions of post-Auschwitz life.

In each stage, however, Wiesel reveals the moral role of literature by fusing art and action in the world on behalf of humanity. All of his second-generation Holocaust witnesses hear tales which describe the reversal of classical paradigms. During the *Shoah*, the Exodus of Redemption became the exodus to oblivion, the *Akedah* did not save one Isaac but murdered one-and-a-half million, and the chosen people were exterminated by the master race. Listening to these tales causes Wiesel's second-generation witnesses to reflect on the meaning of post-Auschwitz Jewish identity and covenantal responsibility. Consequently, the covenantal dimension of his second-generation witnesses resides in several factors: their relationship to the Jewish past, their concern for other Jews, and their determination to transmit the Jewish tale on behalf of humanity in an attempt to limit suffering. Precisely because Wiesel's additional covenant is anchored in the act of testimony, the second generation's compulsion to bear witness with ritual intensity has covenantal implications which are still in the process of unfolding.

NOTES

1. Harry James Cargas, "What is a Jew? Interview with Elie Wiesel," *Responses to Elie Wiesel*, ed. Harry James Cargas (New York: Persea Books, 1978) 157.

2. On novels written by daughters and sons of survivors see Alan L. Berger, "Job's Children: Post-Holocaust Jewish Identity in Second Generation Literature," *Jewish Identity in America*, eds. David M. Gordis and Yoav Ben-Horin (Los Angeles: The University of Judaism, 1991); "Bearing Witness: Second Generation Literature of the *Shoah*," *Modern Judaism* 10 (February, 1990) 1; and "Ashes and Hope: The Holocaust in Second Generation American Literature," *Reflections of the Holocaust in Art and Literature*, ed. Randolph L. Braham (Boulder: Social Science Monographs, 1990).

3. Elie Wiesel, *The Fifth Son*, trans. Marion Wiesel (New York: Summit, 1985) 192. In addition to the above, this article treats Wiesel's second-generation witnesses in three other novels: *The Oath* (New York: Avon Books, 1974); *The Testament*, trans. Marion Wiesel (New York: Summit Books, 1981); and *The Forgotten*, trans. Stephen Becker (New York: Summit, 1992).

4. Ellen Fine, *Legacy of Night: The Literary Universe of Elie Wiesel* (Albany: SUNY Press, 1982) 9.

5. Wiesel's comment is cited in Hillel Goldberg's article "Holocaust Theology: The Survivor's Statement," *Tradition* 20:2 (Summer, 1982) 150.

6. Elie Wiesel, *One Generation After*, trans. Lily Edelman and Elie Wiesel (New York: Schocken Books, 1982) 174.

7. Elie Wiesel, "The Holocaust as Literary Inspiration," *Dimensions of the Holocaust* (New York: Northwestern University and Anti-Defamation League of B'nai B'rith, 1977) 9.

8. Fine 9.

9. Fine 9.

10. Fine 113.

11. Irving Abrahamson, ed. *Against Silence: The Voice and Vision of Elie Wiesel*, 3 vols. (New York: Holocaust Library, III, 1985) 323.

12. Abrahamson 3: 323.

13. Abrahamson 3: 323.

14. Abrahamson 3: 321.

15. Lily Edelman. "A Conversation with Elie Wiesel," *Responses* 18.

16. Fine 130.

17. Michael Berenbaum, *The Vision of the Void* (Middletown: Wesleyan University Press, 1976) 92, 100.

18. Abrahamson 3: 120.

19. Wiesel's critique of Communism sharply distinguishes that totalitarian system from Judaism on both theological and humanistic grounds. Concerning the former he writes, "Communism started out as a movement of compassion, fraternity, and humanity. But it lost its humanity, and it became one of the most vicious, one of the bloodiest, one of the cruelest experiments in history — because it began by denying God entry into history. And the next step was to deny man the right to be in history, freely, independently as a sovereign human being." Abrahamson, *Against Silence* 3: 125.

Concerning Communism's humanistic failure, Wiesel states that "The problem with communism was that it became an experiment of sacrificing living people for the sake of an abstraction. That is something one does not do. You do not take a living human being and sacrifice him today for the sake of another human being who will be born tomorrow. The end does not justify the means. When it comes to human life, every person is an end, not a means." Abrahamson, *Against Silence* 3: 267-268.

These distinctions are essential to Wiesel's notion of bearing witness. One performs this task in order to uphold the sanctity of life.

20. Abrahamson 3: 119.

21. Fine 144.

22. This point is borne out by Wiesel himself. Reflecting on the symbolism of Grisha's muteness, Wiesel states that "The ironic part is that we have given our testimony and our testament to a young generation which is mute, which cannot speak about it. But then, how could one speak about it? We are all mute." *Conversations with Elie Wiesel*, ed. Harry James Cargas (South Bend, Indiana: Justice Books, 1992) 163.

23. Daniel Stern views *The Testament* and *The Fifth Son* collectively as signifying Wiesel's move from despair to hope. Stern writes that "It is possible to see two historical events converging to push a despairing witness, still in thrall to silence, into fresh speech and fresh action. In this respect both issues are related. The slaughtered millions of the Holocaust had endured their fates and were gone, but the fate of the Jews of the Soviet Union and the children of the survivors were both still in question." Daniel Stern, "Elie Wiesel: A Thirty-Year Dialogue Between Hope and Despair," *Elie Wiesel: Between Memory and Hope*, ed. Carol Rittner (R.S.M. New York: New York University Press, 1990) 14. I believe that Stern's point is well taken but that he has not gone far enough in seeing the nature of the dramatic difference of *The Fifth Son* from Wiesel's earlier works. On *The Fifth Son* see Alan L. Berger, *Crisis and Covenant: The Holocaust in American Jewish Fiction* (Albany: SUNY Press, 1985) 68-79.

24. *The Haggadah*, ed. Rabbi Joseph Elias Artscroll Mesorah Series (New York: Mesorah Publications Ltd., 1990) 85.

25. Abrahamson 3: 320

26. On this point see Alan L. Berger's review of *The Forgotten*, "Lest We Forget," *Midstream*, August/September 1992: 43-44.

27. Elie Wiesel, *Report to the President: President's Commission on the Holocaust* (Washington: U.S. Government Printing Office, 1983).

28. Alan L. Berger, "Elie Wiesel," *Interpreters of Judaism in the Late Twentieth Century*, vol. VII (Washington: B'nai B'rith History of the Jewish People, 1993) 375.

29. This theme, first stated in *Night*, runs throughout Wiesel's oceanic writings. To cite but one instance, in *The Gates of the Forest* Wiesel described the Kaddish as a "solemn affirmation, filled with grandeur and serenity, by which man returns God his crown and his scepter" (225).

30. Berenbaum 127.

31. Wiesel defines the Messianism of the unredeemed as being able "to remain human in a world that is inhuman." Abrahamson, 1: 255 and 3: 301. For a rich discussion of this phenomenon see Maurice Friedman's *Abraham Joshua Heschel and Elie Wiesel: You Are My Witnesses* (New York: Farrar, Strauss, Giroux, 1987) Chapter 18.

32. Elhanan in *The Forgotten* expresses Wiesel's view on this matter. He remembers his martyred father saying that "the messianic promise dwells in each of us" (166).

33. Elie Wiesel, "Why I Write,"*Confronting the Holocaust: The Impact of Elie Wiesel,* trans. Rosette C. Lamont, eds. Alvin Rosenfeld and Irving Greenberg (Bloomington: Indiana University Press, 1978) 203-204.

34. The heterogeneity of response to traditional Jewish practice and teaching is even more pronounced when one examines the variety of approaches reflected in novels by daughters and sons of survivors. On this matter see above, note 2.

A Wound That Will
Never Be Healed:
An Interview with Elie Wiesel

by BOB COSTAS

BC: How would you describe Sighet, your childhood home, and what was your childhood like before you were taken from there?

EW: It was a typical *shtetl,* meaning a typical Jewish town. Majority Jewish. Fifteen thousand Jews, some ten thousand non-Jews, but the life was dominated by the Jews, meaning on Saturday, all the shops were closed. On Jewish holidays, even the non-Jews participated somehow in those holidays. My childhood was a happy/unhappy childhood. Happy because I was home with my family, with my teachers, my friends. Profoundly religious. I was profoundly religious, meaning, to me, God was more important than any other person in the world. I was obsessed with it, with study, with prayer — fanatically obsessed. Today, when I think about it, I'm inundated with sadness. I didn't know, for instance, how poor the poor Jews were. Because we had our wealthy people, our poor people; we had people who were bourgeois, those who were very rich. And then when I came back twenty years later, I realized that even the rich were very poor. And yet, it came on a *Shabbat,* on a Saturday, the poverty was gone. People who were coachmen, who were cobblers, tailors, who had difficulties making a living during the week, but the moment the Saturday set in, the Sabbath set in, we had the feeling that a strange metamorphosis occurred, that the profane became sacred.

BC: As Hitler's Gestapo went about its work and reports filtered into that part of Transylvania about the atrocities that were going

An abbreviated version of this interview aired on the *LATER . . . with Bob Costas* television program in two segments on January 13 and 14, 1992, and was repeated on April 13 and 14, 1992. The uncut transcript of the original interview is printed here for the first time by permission of NBC-TV. It has been edited by Jerry Call and Lori Loesche.

on nearby, most people, for one reason or another, according to what I've read of your writings, didn't believe it. Even when a gentleman known as Moché the Beadle came back, having escaped, and tried to warn them, they thought he was mad, right?

EW: Yes. That happened in 1941. The Hungarians were then in control, in power. And in 1941, they decided to deport the so-called foreign Jews, foreign-born Jews. And they were not foreign-born, not more than I, no more than I, but yet they couldn't prove that they were citizens. And they were deported across the border to Galicia, and they were all killed — machine-gunned — and only one escaped, this Moché the Beadle. And he came back. And I loved him. I loved stories, and I loved his stories, too. They were horrible stories, but I loved them anyway. But nobody believed him. Why should they have believed him? He was not an important person, he was a beadle. And everybody was convinced that he had lost his mind. And then he stopped talking altogether because nobody believed him. Therefore, I am so angry at people who knew and didn't tell us. If we had heard — let's say in 1943, even after the Warsaw Ghetto uprising — if we had heard a broadcast by Roosevelt, by Churchill, or by Jewish leaders in Palestine then, or in America, I think we would have taken it seriously. But to take seriously a beadle? Hallucinations. And as a result, when we came in 1944 to Auschwitz, we didn't know what it meant.

BC: So when they first gathered you up and took you from your home, were you actually hopeful? Could you rationalize some possibility, some outcome here, other than death, other than this unthinkable outcome?

EW: We didn't think of death. It happened in March — March 19, 1944, the Germans came into Hungary. Two months or so before the Normandy invasion. The Russians were very near. And then the ghetto arrived. Two weeks later, we were all in the ghetto. At night we would see the artillery exchange between the Russians and the Germans. They were only twenty kilometers away. We could have escaped. There was nothing to prevent us from escaping because there were two Germans, Eichmann and someone else, some fifty Hungarian gendarmes, and there was no problem. We could have left the ghetto into the mountains. We had non-Jewish friends who wanted us to come and stay with them. But we didn't know. We thought the war would end soon, and the Russians would come in, and Hitler would be defeated, and everything would come back to normalcy.

BC: When they loaded you all up and took you out of town, did you think then that this was the end of the line, or did you think that perhaps you would simply be detained for a while and, when the war ended, liberated?

EW: Well, the Germans had developed a psychology, a kind of mass psychology, how to fool, how to deceive the victims. And we were all victims. We didn't know. Until the very last moment, we believed that families would remain together, and we should be in some labor camp. Young people would work, and the parents would stay home and prepare food, meals. We didn't know until the very last minute, until it was too late.

BC: I know that you'll never forget the words "Men to the left, women to the right." That's how they separated you from your mother and your sisters, you and your father.

EW: Well, of course, that was the real shock, the brutality of the words. The words were simple, "left" and "right," but what they meant, the meaning of those words, hit me much later. For three days or so I was in a haze. I thought I was dreaming. For three days I was dreaming. We were there in the shadow of the flames, and to me it wasn't real. I couldn't believe it. I write about it in *Night*. I couldn't believe it that in the twentieth century, in the middle of the twentieth century, people should do that, could do that, to other people. I somehow couldn't accept it, and to this day I cannot accept it. Something in me rejects that notion that would dehumanize a killer to such an extent. And the complicity, the indifference of the world — this, to this day, it moves me to anger.

BC: When they tattooed a number on your arm, was that the single most dehumanizing moment, or is it just one in a litany of dehumanizing moments?

EW: Oh, that didn't mean a thing, but the first dehumanizing incident was the day when we arrived, really. (I mean the next day — we arrived at night.) And there was a Kapo, and my father went to him saying he would like to go to the toilet. And my father was a respectful man. And the Kapo hit him in his face, and my father fell to the ground. That was the beginning of the experience really, that I, his only son, couldn't come to his help. Usually I should have thrown myself at the tormentor and beat him up. But that was the first realization there that he and I were already in prison, and not only I, but my mind is in prison, my soul is in prison, my being is in prison, and I am no longer free to do what I want to do.

BC: Was there talk from time to time of inmates banding together in some kind of revolt which, even if it were to fail, at least would have liberated their spirits from captivity?

EW: There were revolts even at Buchenwald. The *Sonderkommando*, the commander that burned the corpses, that staged the revolt in 1944, they were all killed afterwards. In our camps, both in Auschwitz-Birkenau, where I was, and then Buchenwald, there were members of the resistance. I know that, but I was so young, and I was so timid, that I didn't even know about it. I knew vaguely that some people are members of an underground organization because they hanged a few.

BC: What were the most conspicuous examples of heroism, under the circumstances, that you saw, and were there examples of cowardice that you saw among the captive Jews?

EW: Cowardice is a word that we didn't apply because, logically, everyone should have been a coward — could have been and probably was because one SS man with a machine gun was stronger than a thousand poets. Heroism . . . I've seen heroism, a spectacular kind of heroism, which I described when three members of the underground were hanged, and the way they faced the execution was heroic. But then I've seen heroism in a simple way. Let's say a man who would come to us on the Sabbath — I don't even know his name — and would simply say, "Don't forget that today is *Shabbat*." Don't forget that today is Sabbath. To us it meant nothing, because how could it? Same thing, Sabbath, Sunday, Monday. We were all destined to be killed. The fact that he said, "Don't forget that it is the Sabbath, a sacred day." Or somebody would come and say, "Don't forget your name. You are not only a number, you have a name." I've seen people giving their bread to their comrades whom they didn't know. I've seen a person who has offered himself to be beaten up instead of somebody else, whom he didn't know. In general, you know, the enemy, the killers, what they wanted to do there was to dehumanize the victim by depriving him of all moral values. Therefore the first lesson that they gave us was you are alone; don't count on anyone, don't think of anyone, only of yourself. You are alone, and only you should matter to yourself. And they were wrong. Because those who did care for somebody else — a father for his father, a son for his father, a friend for a friend — I think they lived longer because they felt committed, which means humanity became heroic in their own hearts.

BC: As I said, you and your father were separated, as they broke the men and the women apart, from your mother and your sisters, and you would never see your younger sister or your mother again; they perished. The theme of *Night* (your first book) that runs through the whole thing is your father trying to support you, you trying to support your father, at all costs not becoming separated from each other. And then just one of the tragic facts of those years is that your father finally succumbed only months before the U.S. forces liberated the concentration camp.

EW: As long as my father was alive, I was alive. When he died, I was no longer alive. It wasn't life; it was something else. I existed, but I didn't live. And even when we were together we had a certain code. We didn't talk about my mother, my sisters. We didn't talk. We were afraid. There were certain things in those times and in those places that people cannot understand today. We didn't cry. People didn't cry inside that universe. Maybe because people were afraid if they were to start crying, they would never end. But people didn't cry. Even when there were selections and somebody left somebody else, there were no tears. It was something so harsh — the despair was so harsh — that it didn't dissolve itself in tears, or in prayers either.

BC: You saw the reverse, though, too. I mean, you detail situations where a son beat his father because that was the way he thought, at least temporarily, to get into the good graces of his captors; a situation where a younger, stronger son took a morsel of bread from his dying father.

EW: Yes, I've seen, but there were very few, really, in truth, there were few. It's normal. But what happened there, the killers managed to create a universe parallel to our own. The kind of creation, a parallel creation, and there they established their own society with its own rulers, with its own philosophers, its own psychologists, its own poets, with a new society outside God, outside humanity. And, naturally, some succumbed. I cannot even judge them. I cannot be angry at them. Imagine a child of twelve arriving in Auschwitz, and he knows that only violence could be a refuge. Either he becomes an author of violence or a victim of violence. So, a child of twelve overnight aged and became an old person. How can I judge such a child? He didn't do it. He was made to do it by — he was conditioned to do it — by the tormentor. If I am angry, I am angry at the tormentor, not at the victim.

BC: Toward the end of *Night*, you describe your father's death. And he did not go to the furnaces, except to burn his corpse. He died of dysentery and a combination of the hardships.

EW: The hunger. Hunger and exhaustion, fatigue.

BC: And the last night, he was calling out to you for water, but at the same time a guard was beating him. And your best judgment was that you couldn't help him. You were helpless; you didn't respond. And then you write, "There were no prayers at his grave. No candles were lit to his memory. His last word was my name. A summons to which I did not respond." You couldn't possibly feel guilt about that, if you are being hard on yourself.

EW: I do, I do. I do feel guilt. I know that logically I shouldn't, but I do feel guilty because we were terribly close. We became very close there. But, at the same time, the instinct prevented me from being killed. If I had moved, I would have been killed. Beaten up to death. I was as weak as he was. And who would have known that he would die that night? And we didn't know. But I do feel guilty.

BC: You saw a child, who you described as having the face of an angel — saw that child hanged. That's one of the most moving passages in the book. This is (obviously you have steeled yourself) your life's work, to tell of these things, so that's why I feel no reluctance to ask you to tell again, but how does somebody watch these things — these things unthinkable if we read them in fiction — unfold and then find some reason to keep on living?

EW: Well, first, you know, I don't speak about this often. I have written a few books, very few. I prefer, I think, books on the Talmud and the Bible. And through them, I transmit certain obsessions, certain fears, or certain memories. At that time it was my father who kept me alive. We saw it together. And I wanted him to live. I knew that if I die, he will die. And that was the reason I could eat after having seen that scene, the hanging. And I remember it well, I remember it now. I didn't forget a single instant, a single episode.

BC: Did you assume, as you and your father tried as best you could to survive, that your mother and your sister were dead?

EW: Oh, we knew, but we didn't talk about it. I knew. He knew. At one point only, the very first night, when we were walking toward the flames — we didn't know yet anything, but we were walking toward the flames — my father said, "Maybe you should have gone with your mother." Had I gone with my mother, I would have been killed that night too. But we never talked about this. There was a kind of rule: we don't talk about it, about those who are absent, because it hurts too much. We couldn't accept such pain.

BC: Everyone, except those deranged and hateful souls who try to propound this preposterous theory that the Holocaust didn't occur, knows it occurred, and, statistically, they understand the dimensions of it. But until one hears the stories of Holocaust survivors and just a tiny number of the hundreds of thousands of particulars, until you hear that, you can't begin to grasp the ghastly horror of it. There is just no way, if you stood on a mountaintop for five thousand years and screamed to the top of your lungs, to overstate it.

EW: We cannot *overstate* it. We must *understate* it. To make it understandable, we must understate it. That's why in this little book, *Night*, which has few pages actually, what I *don't* say is important, as important as the things that I *do* say. But even if you read all the books, all the documents, by all the survivors, you would still not know. Unfortunately, only those who were there know what it meant being there. And yet we try. One of my first goals, really, was to write for the survivors. I wanted them to write. In the beginning we didn't speak. Nobody spoke. We felt, who would understand? Who would believe? And why talk? And, really, the main reason for writing *Night* was not for the world or for history; it was for them. Look, it's important to bear witness. Important to tell your story. At the same time I know that even if all the stories were to be read by one person — the same person — you would still not know. You cannot imagine what it meant spending a night of death among death.

BC: Smelling burning flesh . . .

EW: The flames . . .

BC: . . . of being in the back of a wagon . . .

EW: . . . seeing . . .

BC: . . . with corpses . . .

EW: . . . seeing the flames . . .

BC: . . . all around you.

EW: . . . seeing the flames first of all, seeing the flames and smelling the smell. And knowing that it depends on the whim of an *SS* man. He didn't have to explain. Just capricious gesture. And that's it.

BC: Did you ever see any humanity in the actions or in the eyes of your captors, any humanity at all?

EW: I did not.

BC: How do you suppose it is possible to purge humanity from so many people?

EW: Bob, this is the question of my life. After the war, I had a series of shocks, and one of the shocks was when I discovered that the commanders of the so-called *Einsatzkommando*, that did firing in Eastern Europe, meaning in the Ukraine and Russia, had college degrees. Some of them had Ph.D.s, and that, to me, an educator — I am a professor, I teach, I write — I can't understand it. What happened? Culture is supposed to be a shield, a moral shield. What happened to the shield? I don't understand that to this day.

BC: To murder children, to use them for bayonet practice in front of their parents.

EW: I don't understand that to this day. How is it possible? How come they didn't go mad? Morally mad if not mentally insane? But they did it, and for them it was a game. I am trying to understand this, so, I say to myself, maybe they tried to push the limits of cruelty farther and farther beyond the horizon. We are trying to push the limits of intelligence, of culture, of humanity, farther and farther, to broaden the scope, to broaden the realm of humanity, and they tried the opposite, which means they believed in a kind of God of evil. And, therefore, Hitler was a prophet of evil. And, therefore, they made an experiment. What can they obtain through evil? How far can they go in evil? But I don't understand.

BC: You came face to face with Dr. Joseph Mengele, who wore a monocle, carried a baton in his hand, an almost theatrical looking character. Can you describe him beyond that?

EW: He used to sing opera while he was doing what he was doing. He would sing melodies from opera. I heard it later on, really, from people who worked with him, inmates. He was an intelligent man, intellectual, polite. He even developed friendships with Jews, or with Gypsy children. There was a Gypsy camp, and he got fond of one of the Gypsy children, and his fondness then was translated in his own personal care of him: he took him to the gas chamber. The young Gypsy child whom he loved and caressed and embraced and kissed. I don't understand what happened to humanity, in the human being. I don't know.

BC: You mentioned that your life was a very religious life, devoted to the study of the Talmud. And you write of a point in this experience, where you say, "I was the accuser, God the accused. My eyes were open and I was alone — terribly alone in a world without God, and without man. Without love or mercy. I had ceased to be anything but ashes, yet, I felt myself to be stronger than the Almighty, to whom my life had been tied for so long. I stood amid a praying congregation, observing it like a stranger." You were spiritually and emotionally a dead person at the age of fifteen.

EW: But I kept on praying nevertheless. What I write here is a protest, and I believe in protest. I still believe in protest, even in protest against God. But what I felt then is true. But it was not a feeling of separation from God, meaning that I stopped believing in God. I protested against the injustice of God or the absence of God in the universe, in history. But even then I kept on believing.

BC: You never stopped believing?

EW: I had a crisis of faith after the war, not during. I came back, I came to France after the war. I reopened my religious life. I became as religious as before. And only later I began studying philosophy, and I worked, I worked in myself, and I had a crisis, a very serious crisis of faith.

BC: How long did it last, and how was it resolved?

EW: A few years. What saved me was my passion for study. I love to study. And even when I had a crisis, I kept on studying. It wasn't totally dissolved because even today I keep on asking questions, and there are no answers.

BC: A question which every kid with a high school education has heard, even one who's given scant thought to philosophy, is, if there is a God, how does God allow something like a Holocaust to happen?

EW: I don't know. If there is an answer, it is the wrong answer. But you see it's wrong, I think, to put everything on God's shoulders. That is something I understood later. Where was man? Where was humanity? Look, after all, we had faith in humanity — I had faith in humanity. To us, President Roosevelt was more important than Ben-Gurion. I had never heard of the name of Ben-Gurion in my little town. But I knew the name of Roosevelt. I remember we said prayers for him. He was the father of the Jewish people. He knew. Absolutely he knew. And yet he refused to bomb the railways going to Auschwitz. Why? Had he done that — at that time, during the Hungarian deportation, ten thousand Jews were killed every day in Auschwitz. Even if the Germans had tried to repair the rail . . .

BC: So even as the U.S. waged war against the Axis powers, you're saying they didn't do enough to hit the specific targets. They could have stopped that cold.

EW: They could have. Look . . . they . . . I admire the American soldiers who fought Hitler, and I think we should be eternally grateful to them, to their families, to their children, to their parents. Many died in the war. They were heroes. But somehow the war that Hitler had waged against the Jewish people was forgotten. In the process. And that was wrong. A few bombing operations would have at least shown Hitler that the world cared. Hitler was convinced to the end that the world didn't care about what he and his acolytes had done to the Jewish people.

BC: So even as the war turned against them and they were losing the war, almost to the last, they continued executing Jews. They continued their torture.

EW: Oh sure. Even at the end, trains carrying Jews to death had priority over military trains taking soldiers to the front. It was crazy. When you think about it, it's totally crazy. But that was their logic.

BC: Do you recall what you saw and what you felt the day the troops liberated Buchenwald in April of 1945?

EW: It was April 11, 1945, in the morning hours. We were the last remnants in Buchenwald, and I had been already at the gate almost every day. And, by accident, really, by chance, that the gate closed in front of me. So I came back to the camp. I remember when they came in. We were then already terribly hungry, more than usual because no food was given to us for six days, since April 5th. And I remember the first American soldiers. I remember black soldiers. I remember a black sergeant, huge. And then he saw us; he began sobbing and cursing. He was so moved by what he saw that he began sobbing — he sobbed like a child, and we couldn't console him. And we tried somehow to console him, and that made him sob even deeper, stronger, louder. So I remember those soldiers, and I have a weak — a soft spot — for the American soldier, really. I gave a lecture a few years ago at West Point, and it was amusing to me. I never had any military training or military affinity, and I came to give a lecture, and I told them what I felt about the American uniform, because that meant not only victory, it meant a triumph, the triumph of humanity. And to me, that black sergeant incarnates that triumph.

BC: Toward the end of *Night,* you write about looking into a mirror. Apparently, you didn't have any access to a mirror for two years. What did you see when you looked into that mirror?

EW: Well, when the Americans came in they threw us food, and it was the wrong thing to do because they should have used medical supervision, and they didn't. And I remember I picked up a can, some dessert, something with ham in it. Now during the camp, I would have eaten anything, but I was already free, and my body knew it even before I did, and I put it to my lips and passed out, literally; I got some blood poisoning. So, I woke up in a hospital, a former SS hospital which was taken over by the Americans for inmates. So, I almost died. I was, I think, closer to death after the liberation than before. And then one day, really, I saw myself in that mirror. And I saw a person who was ageless, nameless, faceless. A person who belonged to another world, the world of the dead.

BC: If you belonged to the world of the dead (especially after your father slipped away from you only several weeks before the liberation came, which — the sad irony — just adds to the heartache), if you were dead inside at that point, from where did you summon the strength to direct a life so purposeful in the ensuing forty-plus years?

EW: In the beginning it was again, I repeat, a passion for study. I studied. I came to France together with four hundred youngsters, children, orphans, invited by DeGaulle. And we were taken over by an organization in a children's home, an orphans' home. And the first thing I did, when I came there, I asked for pen and paper. I began writing my memoirs. And for quotations of the Talmud to study. It's later that I developed that since I am alive, I have to give meaning to my life. Oh, it may sound, you know, bombastic, but it is true. That is how I switched. That means that my life as it is, if it is only for myself, then it is wrong. I have to do something with it. I even have to do something with my memory of my death.

BC: Apart from the physical horror, the murders, the torture, the hunger, the separation from loved ones, and then the ultimate loss of loved ones, is there any way to describe what it does to you psychologically to see people that you admire and respect rendered impotent and stripped of their identity, to see that all your mother could do for your little seven-year-old sister was to stroke her hair? That was all, in that circumstance, she could muster to protect her child.

EW: That is a wound that will never be healed. But my father was helpless to protect me. That moment was to me probably the hardest in the entire period. Oh, I have seen professors, famous people, wealthy people, who had connections, who had a purpose in life, who had prestige, social status, and when they entered that universe they became objects like me. That is when I understood that something happened. A mutation. A mutation on the scale of being, that possessions meant nothing, what meant — I don't know what meant — violence. The choice really was to join the sadists, the executioner or to be, to remain, a victim.

BC: And yet there were moments where humanity surfaced in such a shining, even if tragic, fashion. You mentioned the people going to the gallows without outward complaint and then, as a last word, saying, "Long live liberty." Or people volunteering to be beaten in place of another.

EW: What a price. What a price, to die for a few words.

BC: There is a passage here that is extraordinarily moving. There are a group of you loaded into a wagon, and many have died. It is a bitter winter, and there are sick people literally in amongst the corpses, in some cases being nearly smothered by the corpses. And there was a young man who had a violin.

EW: Juliek.

BC: "It was pitch dark. I could hear only the violin, and it was as though Juliek's soul were the bow. He was playing his life. The whole of his life was gliding on the strings — his lost hopes, his charred past, his extinguished future. He played as he would never play again. And of course this playing was banned." He could have been killed merely for playing the violin. Especially for playing Beethoven on the violin, which the Germans found especially vile, coming from a Jew. I shall never forget him. "How could I forget that concert, given to an audience of dying and dead men! To this day, whenever I hear Beethoven played, my eyes close and out of the dark rises the sad, pale, face of my Polish friend, as he said farewell on his violin to an audience of dying men. I do not know for how long he played. I was overcome by sleep. When I awoke, in the daylight, I could see Juliek, opposite me, slumped over, dead. Near him lay his violin, smashed, trampled, a strange, overwhelming little corpse."

EW: You know, I used to play the violin before. I played well. And I haven't touched the violin since because of that.

BC: You were reunited with at least one sister, maybe two.

EW: Two.

BC: Two older sisters, by luck.

EW: Yeah, by luck. We were in that orphans' home, and after all four hundred children from Buchenwald, there was a story. The journalists came, and I had never seen a journalist in my life. I had never read the paper in my life. I didn't know who they were. And they spoke to me in German, and I answered in Yiddish. And they took a picture of me. I was playing chess with a friend, and a week later I was in the office of the director of that orphans' home. And I came to ask him about the Talmud. Had he received the book that I wanted? And I heard him speak on the telephone, mentioning my name. And I was too shy — I am a shy person. So I waited until he finished, and then I said, "Is it the Talmud?" He said, "What do you mean?" I said, "You were speaking about me." "Oh, no," he said, "your sister called." I said, "What? My sister? I don't have a sister." And then he realized — it's traumatic — he tried to call back, but they told him that the person who called had called from the post office because she didn't have a telephone. And he said, "She's waiting for you tomorrow in Paris." And for the whole day I was convinced it cannot be. And I came to Paris, and it was my oldest sister. She came to France with another man who was also in camp in Dachau, and they met after liberation, few days, and decided to get married. So she came with him to Paris. And one day she opened the paper; she saw my picture in it. And then we found the other sister, too, who went back to my hometown thinking maybe I was alive. And so, I met the two, and one of them died of cancer in the meantime. The middle one.

BC: There are too many things that have happened, even specific incidents, to touch on them all, but another ironic aspect to your life is that you are a free man; you are in New York City sometime in the '50s, I guess, and you are hit by a car.

EW: Yes.

BC: Thrown, or bounced around, by the impact for almost a block, your body broken, very near death, and somehow you came back from that experience as well.

EW: Oh, but that made me laugh, really. I wanted to laugh. To survive Auschwitz and die of an accident in New York was too much. It was a few weeks after I arrived. It was 1956. And I came in the evening to the New York Times to buy a paper and then to go and file a cable to the paper for which I worked, an Israeli paper, a very poor paper then. (Now it is very rich. Since I left it, it became rich.) And it, a taxi, ran over me. What seems today so unheard of, they brought me to the hospital (I think to one hospital; I won't mention it because otherwise they will sue you), and they checked my pockets, and they realized that I have no money and I am a refugee. They refused to take me. They put me back in the ambulance, and the ambulance went from one hospital to the other looking for a hospital that would take me. Finally they did go to the New York Hospital, and there the chief orthopedic surgeon, named Paul Braunstein, took me in, and he saved my life. I was days in a coma, and for a whole year, almost, I was in and out of hospitals.

BC: At that point was it possible to say to yourself — and this is so much easier for someone like me to theorize than for someone to do in the midst of the experiences that you've had — but did the thought cross your mind, "I'm some sort of superman?"

EW: No.

BC: "I'm here to overcome the obstacles?"

EW: Not really, not me. I'm not a superman. I was always, always weak and always shy, and I don't take initiatives. If I have to speak to somebody, I blush ten times. I am not that kind of person, really. That's why my sisters were convinced I died, because I was always sick when I was a child. And I would have been, really, the natural candidate for death. So, here too, oh, no, I felt it had to happen to me again, really.

BC: You have been involved in a number of humanitarian causes through the years, and that, combined with your writing, led to the Nobel Prize for Peace in the mid-1980s and the single incident which most Americans would most associate you with: you come to the White House, President Reagan gives you a humanitarian award, but he's on his way in a few weeks to Bitburg to lay a wreath at the cemetery, and it's true that some Holocaust survivors, I guess, are buried there, but so too are officers of the SS.

EW: No Holocaust survivors there, only military, German military men, and SS people, SS men. Reagan — I have a soft spot for Reagan, too. He was a warm person, really. Except he relied too much on his advisors, and they told him to go. What I did, I sent him my speech beforehand — respect for the office of the President, after all. I sent him my speech. They behaved in the White House in a terrible way. I got the Congressional Gold Medal, which is the highest honor an American can get, you know. It's a very nice thing. And, by chance, the date was set for April 19. They could have had it in February, so the whole speech would not have taken place. Once they realized that Bitburg was coming, and I went to the White House without publicity, simply warning them, "Don't do it, because it will create a scandal," they didn't want to hear about it. Then, because of that, they decided to play low-key. And the ceremony was supposed to have taken place in the East Room, a hundred fifty people on my side, many members of Congress that I knew and friends, and a hundred fifty for the President. The last three days, three days before, they changed the room for the smallest room in the White House! And they hoped, you know, nobody would notice it and so forth. Little did they know it was going to be live broadcast on television and so forth. But I saw him even before. The day of the ceremony, I went to him, and I saw him, and I pleaded with him; I said, "Mr. President, don't do it. Don't go. You will be the hero. If, after my speech" (because you have to have the ceremony; you cannot go back on it) "you come and you say, 'Alright I'm not going,' you will be the hero all over the world." So one of his advisors said, "Yes, but not in Germany." I said, "So what? You go call up Chancellor Kohl and explain it to him. He will understand. You will make it up." But he didn't. And the funny part was, really, after my address they called me in, one of his senior advisors, senior staff members, that the President wants me to go with him, to go with him on Air Force One to Europe. And I thought that means he is not going to Bitburg, and my only concern was for my coming back: I have to teach in Boston, Boston University. So, I ask, "Alright, and then what?" He said, "You'll go to Bonn, and you'll go to Paris." I said,

"And then what?" And he said, "You'll quickly go to Bitburg."
I said, "What? I don't want *him* to go. You want *me* to go?" To
show you that they didn't have the faintest notion of what the
whole thing was about, the history in it.

BC: He thought, I guess, if you would accompany him, that it
would be some sort of gesture of goodwill or reconciliation. He
just didn't grasp the issues.

EW: The people around him — they had no idea of the historic
implications, really.

BC: Then you saw him again, about a year later at the Ellis Island
ceremonies, when they unveiled the new Statue of Liberty or the
repaired Statue of Liberty?

EW: Then, there were, I think, ten or twelve foreign-born Americans
who got these Liberty Medals. Kissinger, myself and Itzhak Perlman.
And it was awkward, a little bit, because once again he was giving
me a medal. Different circumstances. It was nice anyway. It was
a nice feeling.

BC: So you have no antagonism toward him?

EW: No, of course not. I feel for him. I feel sorry for him because
it was the lowest point of his Presidency. And he could have
avoided it. He deserves better than that, really, to remain in history
linked to Bitburg.

BC: You had been to the Soviet Union in the mid-'60s, and you
wrote a book called *The Jews of Silence.* Of course everyone knows
at that time the circumstances: no possibility to emigrate, no
possibility to openly practice their religion. Now a much different
set of circumstances, and you saw Gorbachev either very close to,
or almost right in the middle of, the recent upheaval, right?

EW: I saw him a few hours after he came back from his house
arrest. I was sent there by President Francois Mitterand. He and
I have been friends from before he was president. And he called
me, and he gave me his presidential plane to go to Moscow and
bring a personal message to Yeltsin and Gorbachev of support and
so forth. So I saw Gorbachev.

BC: What do you feel, in brief terms, is the future of Soviet Jewry?

EW: When I was there in '65, nobody knew about their tragedy. People didn't even know about their resistance. I was convinced I won't find Jews there — a few thousand Jews here and there. And when I came and I went to Kiev all I saw was fear, fear, fear. Everybody, but also Jewish fear. And then came a holiday called Simchath Torah, the Celebration of the Law, and I came to the synagogue in Moscow, and there were thousands and thousands and thousands of youngsters who came out with their musical instruments singing their allegiance to the Jewish people. And that was for me the beginning of the realization that they want to be Jewish, and they are free, they want to be free. Before Solzhenitsyn and before Sakharov and before the other dissidents, these youngsters defied the Kremlin and its terror. And so, then, I began really in '65 working for Soviet Jewry and the dissidents too, but they were the focus. I have faith in the Soviet Jews. I have faith in humanity in general in spite of everything else, and yet I have faith that many will leave, of course; many want to leave, but those who will remain will remain Jews.

BC: Did you ever, subsequent to Auschwitz, come face to face with Gestapo officers?

EW: No.

BC: Former Nazis? Not once?

EW: No. I came face to face, and I wrote about it in one of my books, in Israel, during the Eichmann trial. I saw Eichmann at the trial, but he was in a glass cage. But later, I saw, in a bus, going from Tel Aviv to Jerusalem, a man that I — I recognized his neck. He was a kind of blockhouse, or barracks, head in Auschwitz. My barracks head. And I passed him, and all of a sudden I said, "Tell me, where were you during the war?" And he said, "Why?" And I said, "Aren't you a German Jew? Weren't you in Poland?" He said, "Yes." "Weren't you in Auschwitz?" "Yes." "In the barracks?" "Yes." I gave him the number, at which point he paled because had I said, "You were a head of a barracks," they would have beaten him up during the Eichmann trial, and for a few seconds, I became his judge. Literally, I had his fate in my hands. And then, I decided, I am not a judge; I am a witness. I let him go.

BC: You understand, of course, the passion that fuels the work of so-called Nazi hunters. But your position has been different. Yours is to bear witness . . .

EW: Yes.

BC: . . . rather than to exact revenge or even pursue justice.

EW: Well, pursue justice, yes. But it's not my doing; I cannot do that. I admire those people who are doing it very well, and there are several of these young people, young people who dedicate their lives for the pursuit of justice, and all honor is due them. But my work is something else. I write. I teach. And I bear witness in my way. That doesn't mean I'm better, not at all, or worse. I don't think so. Except we all have our area of competence and activity.

BC: To you, what is happiness?

EW: A child.

BC: And yet you had no childhood. Once the Nazis came, you had no childhood anymore.

EW: Yes, but I was happy until then. I was very happy, meaning I knew the answers to all the questions. I knew I had a home. I had friends. I had teachers. I had God. I had happiness in my childhood. And, therefore, when I think of the past, what hurts most is when I think that a million Jewish children were killed, and since then, when I see a child, I go to pieces. Any child.

BC: What are your thoughts about your own son, who now is nearly twenty, I guess? When he was a small child, the innocence you saw in him must have been overwhelming.

EW: I'll tell you, my son and I have such a strange, marvelous, great relationship that he would not want me to speak about him. You will forgive me if I don't because he wouldn't like it.

BC: Is the God you believe in a God who exacts revenge?

EW: No, although we are told in the Psalms that God is a God of revenge. But I don't believe it. God is, as a philosopher said, God is patient. The whole problem of theodicy — Why are the just punished and the wicked rewarded? — is answered in that line, that God is patient. What seems bad today, tomorrow is not so bad. And even if a person is happy today, the wicked person, tomorrow he won't be, or she won't be. So I don't think God is revengeful. God is truth. And when I speak of redemption in my books, it is the redemption of truths.

BC: Do you believe in hell?

EW: Sure. Here, not there.

BC: So you don't believe, as some, I guess, would, that there is a hell where, literally or figuratively, a Hitler is consumed in flames.

EW: Oh, there are not enough flames for Hitler. Do I believe in the afterlife? That's a different question, a difficult question — it's so complicated. You know, when does it begin? And who? And what? But I believe there is afterlife here, meaning a person can lead more than one life by committing himself or herself to certain causes. If I try to help another person, I think I would like to live his or her life or join my life to their life. So it is possible to have an afterlife even while being alive.

BC: Do you believe in the possibility, or at least hope for the possibility, of reconciliation with your father, your mother, your little sister?

EW: Reconciliation in my memory, yes. But reconciliation meaning physically afterwards? For a while, for many years, I was tempted. I was seduced by them. At one point, I even considered suicide, thinking that they are waiting for me. But I belong to a tradition that believes in life, and, in the eyes of that tradition, whatever is death is impure. Whatever is life is sacred.

BC: Do you expect an explanation, either through revelation here or if there is an afterlife? Do you expect that you might be able to get a full explanation?

EW: Oh, I would like to get it, but I also know I can only get it for myself. That is kind of a Buddhist attitude. The self, the eternal self, the dharma, as the Buddhists call it. For one period in my life I was taken by Buddhism. At that time, I was in India. Whatever I have to find, I know I can find it in the ancient texts. That's why I study Talmud and study the Bible and study Hasidism. I believe in mysticism. I love mystic literature. So whatever is is there.

BC: Does suffering confer moral authority on a person?

EW: Oh, no. Suffering confers no privileges. And, therefore, when people say, "I suffer, therefore . . ." Nonsense. Other people also suffer, and I have no right to measure my suffering against anyone else's suffering. It all depends what I do with that suffering. If I use it to help other people to avoid suffering, then I may have some moral authority, but if I use it in order to increase other people's suffering, then I abuse it, and I have no authority whatsoever.

BC: Please, don't think for a moment that this question is intended to trivialize the most important aspects of your experience, but I think people who admire you would wonder about it. Are there moments of gaiety and spontaneous laughter in your life, or is the enormity of this experience such that it is always with you, that there is a certain solemnity about you at all times?

EW: Oh, no, no. Really not. I laugh, and I am happy, and I love good concerts, and I love my good friends, and we tell jokes to each other. And then I give lectures at the Y, for instance, or at Boston University. I try to introduce as much humor . . . no, I am not a person who believes in macabre or serious despairing moods. Nonsense. I don't have the right to impose that upon anybody else. The opposite: I like good cheer and good theatre and good comedies, and, in general, I think life is not only tears. Life also has happiness to offer and to receive.

BC: Do you worry that as Jewish culture becomes less distinct, at least here in America, and there are pockets of exceptions to that in the Hasidic community, or whatever, but as Jewish culture becomes less distinct and as generational memory blurs as we move further and further from the Holocaust, that the meaning of this will slip further into the ash heap of history, and as witnesses grow older and perish . . .

EW: I do worry. I am not afraid that the event will be forgotten. There were many years in my life that I was afraid that it will be, might be, forgotten. And, therefore, I try to work. I try to inspire and to convince many of my friends also to work. Now I know it won't be forgotten because there are enough documents and books and pictures and even masterworks that will prevent people from forgetting. Today, if I am afraid, and I am afraid, it is that the event will be trivialized, cheapened, reduced to commercial kitsch. That is a source of anguish.

BC: Are all, or almost all, theatrical treatments, movies, stage productions that deal with the Holocaust an affront to you, or can some of them help to illuminate that experience?

EW: Not all, no. Some can. And some do. But the big extravaganzas, I'm afraid, offended many of us.

BC: Could it ever happen again?

EW: No, I don't think that the Holocaust can ever happen again, meaning the real event, meaning when a state is taken over by a group of fanatics and that group establishes the law, the law of death. But what Germany induced and made other people endure was that it was legal to kill Jews. I don't think it can happen, meaning to establish ghettos and then concentration camps with gas chambers, the whole technique, the technology, the technique of killing, of mass killing, cannot happen. Unless we forget. If we forget, then the forgetting itself would be a tragedy and a crime equal to the tragedy and the crime of those years.

BC: Does it bother you when the word "pogrom" is perhaps misused, trivialized?

EW: Sure.

BC: A recent example (and I am sure that there are many), we have the situation in Crown Heights, where there is undoubtedly a huge strain of anti-Semitism involved and where Jews have been subjected to mistreatment, to hatred and, in a couple of cases, to murder, but it seems to me that even while you decry that, one can certainly make a distinction between that and a pogrom, which is a pogrom that has government sanction and is much more systematic than hatred itself.

EW: I agree. I didn't like the word, but then there is a devaluation of many words. A person, let's say, killed eight or nine people, and they call him a mass murderer. Mass murder means something. That doesn't mean that I condone, of course. That is serial murder. It's a good, good word. Why call him mass murderer? Take for example a TV sportscaster speaking about the team that lost, and the commentator said it was a "holocaust" on the field. Now, really. So this kind of devaluation, of cheapening, of reduction

— a reductionist attitude — it is, of course, dangerous.

BC: Earlier you spoke of the face of the black sergeant that you saw so vividly when the concentration camp was liberated in April of 1945. And historically, Jews have been on the side of the American civil rights movement.

EW: Oh, yes, yes.

BC: How much does it pain you to see the conflict, which is by no means universal (but it exists) between blacks and Jews in New York these days?

EW: It is painful because we are two minorities, and both of them were victimized quite some time. Just today, we had a meeting at the *New York Times* with a group of important people to discuss black and Jewish, to discuss the issue, to see what can be done. Because it is painful, it is scandalous, philosophically scandalous. That shouldn't happen. All kinds of suggestions were made, and, soon, you will hear about them. What to do to bring these two communities together. They must come together.

BC: Do Jews frequently come to you, whether they are Holocaust survivors themselves or they are descendents of Holocaust survivors, and tell you that their faith has failed them?

EW: Yes, very often. Children of survivors, or survivors themselves. But the other way around, too. People come to me saying, "You know, I was not a believer, but then I became a believer." And both are good. If a person comes to me and says, "I used to be a believer, and because of what I saw, I stopped believing," I embrace him. If a person comes and says, "I was not a believer, now I am," I also embrace him. What I don't like is to meet a person who says, "I was a believer before; I am a believer now." It didn't change. Or a disbeliever. That means that if the event had no effect, then something is wrong with that person.

BC: Do the recitations of the events you lived through, such as those you shared with us earlier, do they ever take on a rote quality for you because you've been asked about them in one form or another so many ways? Or are they always vivid in the retelling each time, even if it is five thousand times?

EW: Bob, this is the second time I speak about all that. I don't like to speak about it. In my courses at the university, I don't teach Holocaust literature. When I *was* teaching it, I had to because nobody else did or very few did twenty, twenty-five years ago. But since then, I don't teach. I teach philosophy and literature, Shakespeare and Socrates, and Hasidism, but not Holocaust. And I don't speak about it. And I must confess to you that even today, I thought you were going to speak about *Sages and Dreamers*, about . . .

BC: And we will . . .

EW: . . . Talmud but not about the Holocaust because I don't like to speak about it. This is the second time. Once I did it, I think, with Bill Moyers, and now with you. So, in all these years, not about the Holocaust, not about my experiences.

BC: And yet you've always said that it's important that you bear witness, that you give some human face to the dimension of this tragedy.

EW: So I have done it with my few books; that means that out of thirty-six books that I have written, I think four or five deal with that subject. And I think it's enough. I'm really too timid. And it's too personal. It costs too much. And I remember I testified at the Barbie trial, although I was not a French victim; I came from Hungary. But all the lawyers and the prosecuting attorneys wrote me a petition I should come and give a kind of general . . . and I remember what it meant to appear there and speak about my little sister. I cannot . . .

BC: At least once in this conversation, but I think only once, you used the word "hatred." No one could blame anybody who was even witness to this, let alone victim of it (and you were both) for hating everybody involved. But hate can consume a person as they move through their life. How have you subdued it or channeled it?

EW: At times I missed it, I wanted it. There were times when I even wrote; I said, we need some kind of hatred. It's normal, it's natural, to channel this hate out, to drive it out, but to *experience* it. Why I didn't — during the war I had other problems on my mind. My father. You know, I really didn't *see* the Germans. I saw the Germans as angels of death. I couldn't lift my eyes. It was forbidden to lift my eyes to see a German *SS* because he would kill you. After the war, I had my problems: how to readjust, how to readjust to death. It was more difficult to readjust to death than to life, to see in death an exception to the rule, not the normative phenomenon. It was difficult because we were used to death as a normative experience. We lived in death; we lived with death. And then to think about death as a scandal, as a tragedy — it took me some time. So we had to do so many things, really, after the war, to find myself again, and to find the language, to find a life, to find a destiny, to find a family, that I didn't think about that, about hatred. But I knew that it had to exist because it was on the other side. And that's why, since the Nobel Prize, really, I've devoted years to organize seminars all over the world called "Anatomy of Hate." I want to understand the power, the destructive power, of hate. The masks that hate can put on. The language of hate, the technique of hate, the structure of hate, the fabric of hate, the genesis of hate.

BC: Is there a single insight about that that you've come to, that you feel certain of?

EW: I learned from those who participated in a few of my seminars — psychiatrists — saying that a child, until the age of three, doesn't hate. Children can be taught to hate after they are three years old. That means something.

BC: And yet many, many Nazis obviously weren't indoctrinated into Nazi philosophy until they were adults or adolescents. As you said earlier, some moral training, some education, was within them and yet was reversed and perverted.

EW: Hate is an easy temptation, you know. It is seductive. The hater feels superior. The hater not only has power but has the knowledge of the victim. The hater feels like God because he can do with the hated whatever he, or sometimes she, wants. So it's not surprising that so many people in Germany, and in some occupied countries of Eastern Europe, became anti-Semitic and racist and members of xenophobia. They were taken by hatred. It was good for them. I think that ultimately what they will have to learn, if they haven't learned already, is that hate destroys the hater just as it destroys the hated.

BC: Maybe this is silly — it's obvious to me that you are a humble person — but must you sometimes hold in check a certain disdain that you might feel for people who get bogged down in life's trivialities, people who obsess on their own little adversities, when you have seen things on such an enormous scale that you must have a better overview of things than almost anybody else you encounter?

EW: Disdain is a strong word. I do have some disdain for some people.

BC: Impatience . . . "impatience" might have been the word.

EW: Impatience, no . . . I have, rather, amusement. I am amused. I will give you an example. In the beginning, when I began writing, you know, and let's say somebody wrote a nasty review, in the beginning it hurt terribly that these people don't understand, or for some selfish reasons, what they did for jealousy. Silly. And then I said to myself, really, "So what?" You know. "What else can they do to me?" What the Germans hadn't done already. "What else can happen to me?" So I feel amused that they are playing their little games, that's all.

BC: What was the happiest moment of your life?

EW: The birth of my son.

BC: Who carries your father's name.

EW: My father's name. It was something very special, you know. I kept on looking at him, and for years I literally kept on looking at him. Looking and looking. When he was asleep, poor boy — no, I was looking and looking! And even today, I don't want to — I don't like to embarrass him, but I could look at him for hours.

BC: Is there a danger, understandably, where Jews feel such a connection to Israel and to what it represents that sometimes they might overlook — either Jews or supporters of Israel — might overlook the complexities which we can't get into in detail, but it is a complex situation in the Middle East, and there might be a blind adherence to one hundred percent of what are perceived to be Israel's positions?

EW: I can tell you about myself. I love Israel with all my heart. I don't live in Israel, never did. Why I didn't go to Israel after the war is a problem which one day we may try to explore together, but I didn't go. I remained in France first and then came here, but

I love Israel with all my heart. That doesn't mean I love Israel's positions. I am not supposed to love or hate Israel's positions. My connection to Israel is based on my traumatized childhood. I have seen what happened to Jews when they were weak, when they were instruments of destiny instead of being the creators of destiny. So when I go to Israel, I feel good. Now it doesn't mean that I don't know what is happening. One of my most heartbreaking moments in my career as a teacher was I came to a university in the Middle West — again, I speak always about literature or philosophy or modern philosophy — and after my lecture a young student got up, and he said, "Professor Wiesel, I don't have a question except the following: I was born in what is now Israel, in Jaffa. And I am an Arab. What do you have to tell me?" And I was so taken by him because there was no hate, no anger, simply a human attempt to make a human contact. What do I say, with my past, with my background as a former refugee, to a young man who is a student who is a refugee? But I answered. I said, "Look, again, let's talk." And we talked, and we talked, and we talked. In one of my books I wrote an open letter to a Palestinian, to a young Palestinian, again, trying to establish contact. I was in Israel. I organized a seminar also on hatred at Haifa University, and one afternoon a group of Palestinians surrounded me with the television on, and they asked me, "How come that you don't speak up for us? You should. We are victims. Why don't you speak up for us?" And I said, "Now, look, if you know me," — because they said they know what I am doing, my work — I said, "If you know me, you know what I feel about Israel. And I must understand Israel's fears. And I challenge you: help me dispel those fears. And I will speak for you about your hopes and your rights. And you know I don't play games with words." So, therefore, we established a very good contact again. I think Israel is going through, as you said, complex situations, but I have faith in Israel's generosity nevertheless. If Begin, who was a hardliner, could give up the Sinai, he surprised Sadat. Sadat didn't expect him to give up, to give up so much and so easily. I think that when the time comes, and the time will come soon, I'm an optimist.

Memories of Jerusalem

by ELIE WIESEL

When did I see Jerusalem for the first time? I don't even know. When I visited the city for the first time, it seemed to me that it was not for the first time. At the same time, each visit since then I have had the feeling it is my first visit.

Is there a Jew, a Jewish child, who possesses a different relationship toward the most Jewish city in the world? Rabbi Yehuda Halevi's nostalgic poem celebrates us all: though we find ourselves here and there in the Western world, the Jewish heart is always in the East.

Like many of us, I have wandered to many cities and even settled, as a stranger or as a resident, in several of them. But the love that Jerusalem always awakens in me has no equal.

One can become enthusiastic over the spell of Paris, over the radiance of the Riviera towns, over the dynamism of New York and the many colors of Bombay. But enthusiasm is not love. For a Jew, love is bound to Jerusalem from the beginning.

Before I even began to speak I dreamed of the widow, the daughter of Zion, who sits alone in the Temple of Jerusalem. I would wait for the little goat that was to give me raisins and almonds and then carry me, and all of us, far away to the city where everything breathes *Yiddishkeit,* where even the stones tell tales of wonder in Yiddish about Jewish kings and princes.

Later, as a *cheder* boy, my schoolmates and I would spin childish fantasies about secret cave tunnels in our Carpathian Mountains that would lead us to Eretz Yisrael. One had only to utter the Name and invisible gates would open. In one blink of the eye all temptations would be cast off. One utterance of the Name and the Exile would end, persecution would end, the enemy would be no more, there would be an end to fear. Master of the Universe, where does one get the Name?

Written in 1967, this essay originally appeared in the *Jewish Daily Forward* and was translated from the Yiddish by Irving Abrahamson. It is printed by permission of the author.

Meanwhile, waiting for someone who knew the Name, we would study and review everything that the Torah and the Gemara had to tell us about the land of our fathers. While studying, we seemed to find ourselves in Jerusalem. All the hills, all the little streets, all the buildings looked familiar. Priests and Levites met us with smiles. Talmudic scholars stopped us in the street and asked us to recite our lesson. Students of Talmud pulled us away to hear Hillel the Elder or Rabbi Akiba lecture.

Though far from Jerusalem we lived between its walls.

* * *

After the war, in France, I lived in various children's homes. Emissaries from the Eretz Yisrael would come to teach us Zionist songs. From time to time we would take part in farewell evenings for comrades who were to emigrate to America, South America, Australia, where a sister, an uncle, a grandfather had sponsored them. No one could go to Eretz Israel; there were no certificates. So they went illegally. Suddenly someone would disappear from the study hall and the dining room. No one asked questions. We simply exchanged glances as if to say, "Him too?" No gatherings, no speeches, no mutual agreements to keep in contact. It was all forbidden. Today I regret this. What were we afraid of? If the English had spies, they never reached as far as our children's homes. What then? Probably they wanted to prepare the illegal immigrants spiritually and psychologically.

Perhaps the English truly did have spies at the train stations. One night one of my close friends — his name was Kalman — entrusted his secret to me: several youngsters, himself included, were to go on the *Exodus*. I could not restrain myself. I accompanied them to the railroad depot. Pointing out an elegantly dressed passenger, the emissary whispered to me, "Look — an English agent." A minute later, "See the young woman with the red scarf? She is also a spy."

When the English sent the *Exodus* back to France, Kalman returned to our circle. To try again? In between, the U.N. voted to establish a Jewish state. And all of us ran to one of the mobilization centers in Paris. The doctor instantly rejected me. And I remained only with a dream.

Reading in French David Ben-Gurion's first speech as prime minister, I barely managed not to break into tears.

* * *

It took a whole year, until the summer of 1949, before I had the opportunity to go to Eretz Yisrael. A Paris newspaper agreed to send me there as a correspondent. My assignment: to portray the life of the new immigrants to the new — yet old — land, theirs and ours.

Naturally, I immediately ran to Jerusalem. The city was still divided. The Old City belonged to Jordan. I spent long hours in the tower of the YMCA building facing the King David Hotel, unable to satisfy myself with the picture of the true Jewish Jerusalem, so near and yet so far.

It was peculiar: the average Israeli citizen hardly missed the Old City. I seldom heard anyone speak of the deep longing that must dominate every Jew who reminds himself of the Kotel Hamaarivi, the Western Wall. How could one go on with his daily activities in the new Jerusalem when the old Jerusalem was in captivity? No one could answer this question for me. The truth is, one gets used to everything.

Each year I would come to Israel for several weeks. The central point of my visit was always to make a pilgrimage to Jerusalem. The road was then still long and difficult. The trip would take two hours. I would become silent during the last twenty minutes. Lost in memories and thoughts, I would come closer to the towers of Jerusalem. My heart would begin to beat quickly, wildly, as though before an encounter with a friend and protector I had not seen in many years — two thousand years. Pictures, forgotten and forever fresh, remained in my fevered brain. Comrades of long ago. My grandfather in his Sabbath kaftan. The Borsher Rebbe and his radiant face. A Jew does not come to Jerusalem totally alone; figures that have influenced his fate always accompany him.

* * *

June 1967. Exactly like many other Jews, I also feared the outcome of the war between Israel and her neighbors. Too many elements reminded me of historic betrayals committed by the world with respect to our people. The enemy openly threatened annihilation, and in the U.N. no one responded. Ahmed Shukheiry, the leader of the Arab terror groups, clearly announced that after this war there would no longer be a Jewish problem. Nasser's soldiers prepared to annihilate or enslave all the Jewish inhabitants of the Jewish state. All the governments knew this. Yet it occurred to no one to warn the Arab leaders that the civilized world would not remain indifferent if they attempted to fulfill their murderous plans.

Therefore we Jews in the Diaspora lived in fear. For the first time since the Holocaust I was afraid that what had happened once was possible again: the Israeli army would fight with the utmost heroism, but without help it would not be able to overcome so many Arab armies that had received all types of modern weapons from Soviet Russia. I know: today we know those fears to have been groundless. It is not our fault. We European Jews have learned that it is wiser to rely on the enemy's threats than on a friend's promises.

* * *

It is not easy to get a seat on the airplane. All the seats are occupied by Israeli officers recalled to duty. Certain airlines have ceased flying into Lod. Nevertheless, thanks to connections with El Al, I manage to get a seat on a plane from Paris to Israel. After a night on the road, I board the El Al plane. I am the last passenger. They close the doors. We are aloft.

No one speaks. Only the heart speaks, and it hears only its own language. I cannot sleep despite my weariness. It is impossible even to take a nap. Whom will I meet in Israel? Which of my friends and acquaintances are at the front? The pilot gives the usual details of the flying conditions, but no one is interested.

Suddenly, a smiling stewardess approaches me and whispers a secret in my ear: "I know who you are." I blush. Under normal circumstances I would answer, "I have worked a lifetime to discover who I am, and *you* know?!" But I am not in the mood to joke, and certainly not with a pretty girl, a smiling one at that.

Later, when other passengers have left her alone, she again comes over to me: "I have read your book." This troubles me a little. At this time, thank God, I have already published seven or eight books, and she speaks of one. Nevertheless, I do not answer. I thank God she has read at least one of my works. "I want to tell you that your book is the best I have read in my whole life," and she continues smiling. "I can quote whole pages." Well, I thank her for the compliment. I think: it is worth going to Israel every week in order to receive such an honor. The stewardess has not finished. "By the way," she says, "in the third chapter there is a sentence I do not understand, Mr. Schwarz-Bart."

Now everything is clear to me. The stewardess has confused me with Andre Schwarz-Bart, the author of *The Last of the Just*. Embarrassed, I attempt to correct her mistake. She rebuffs my words with a laugh. "I know you are flying incognito," she says. "But you don't have to fool me." My protests are no use. She is convinced that I am not I. So she treats me with extraordinary courtesy, as though I had been a member of a millionaire's club. She brings me coffee and chocolate, fruit and more chocolate, so much so that I almost pray to the Creator for the journey never to end.

But the truth gnaws at me after all. I feel it's not fitting to profit from so many favors on another's account. I call the stewardess and start all over again. "I understand your mistake. First, I am also a bit of a writer. Second, I also write in French. Third, Schwarz-Bart's theme is also mine. Fourth, we have the same publisher in Paris. Fifth, we have the same publisher in America. Sixth, we are the closest of friends. Do you want more? We resemble each other physically. You don't believe me? Even the young typesetter in Paris or New York made a terrible error and printed either his picture on my book, or my picture on his book. Now do you understand?" She stares at me a while, then breaks into a quiet laugh. "Until now," she says, "I was convinced that I knew everything about you. One thing I did not know: that you have a sense of humor."

Well, it is a lost cause. I have lost the debate. It is better to keep still and perhaps take a nap.

One or two hours later, she is back again. This time she has a wicked smile. "I do not know who you are," she begins. "But one thing I do know: you are not Andre Schwarz-Bart." Foolishly, I suddenly want to tease her. "Really?" I ask. "Perhaps you can show him to me." Her answer is sharp and biting. "Gladly. Andre Schwarz-Bart . . . sits there!" I jump out of my seat excitedly. Yes, my friend sits three rows ahead of me. I run to him. His surprise is no less than mine. "What are you doing here?" I ask him like a simpleton. "What are *you* doing here?" he asks me. We want to laugh. We want to cry.

We had both heard the call of Jerusalem.

* * *

I shall never forget my arrival in Jerusalem. The war still raged in the Sinai, but it was only the fate of Jerusalem that caught the imagination of the Jewish people. The Arabs were still shooting from the rooftops, but Jews, in the thousands, ran to the Old City, and no one could stop them.

A bizarre, elemental force had suddenly taken possession of all Jews, rabbis and merchants, yeshiva boys and kibbutznikes, officers and schoolchildren, cynics and artists — all had forgotten everything. Each wanted to be at the Kotel Hamaaravi, to kiss the stones, to cry out prayers or memories. Each knew that on that historic day, in that week, the place of the Jew was at the Temple Mount.

I had the privilege to run with them. I have never run with such an impetus. I have seldom said "amen" with such devotion as when the paratroops, in their exaltation, prayed Minhah. I have never understood the profound meaning of *Ahavat Yisrael*, love of Israel, as I did on that day when I stood, as in a dream, under the burning sun and thought with pride of Jewish existence.

At that time an elderly Jew — I thought he was one of the main characters who had stepped out of one of my novels — remarked to me, "Do you know why and how we defeated the enemy and liberated Jerusalem? Because six million souls took part in our battle."

Then I actually saw what the naked eye seldom sees: souls on fire floated high above us, praying to the Creator to protect them and all of us.

And this prayer itself was also transformed into a soul.

NOTES ON THE CONTRIBUTORS

IRVING ABRAHAMSON received his doctorate from the University of Chicago in 1956. He is the compiler and editor of *Against Silence: The Voice and Vision of Elie Wiesel*, published by Holocaust Library of New York, December 1985. Ten years in preparation, the three volumes of *Against Silence* contain what were then considered the complete, uncollected and unpublished works of Elie Wiesel. Abrahamson has taught English at Roosevelt University, the University of Illinois at Chicago, and the City Colleges of Chicago. He was the Elie Wiesel Research Fellow at Chicago's Spertus College of Judaica and has been an Adjunct Professor there. He is a former special adviser to the United States Holocaust Memorial Council.

ALAN L. BERGER directs the Jewish Studies Program and teaches in the Department of Religion at Syracuse University. He has served as acting chairman of the department, been Visiting Gumenick Chair of Judaica at the College of William and Mary, and is currently acting chairman of the Fine Arts Department at Syracuse. Among the books he has written or edited are *Crisis and Covenant*, *Methodology in the Academic Teaching of the Holocaust*, *Bearing Witness to the Holocaust*, and *Judaism in the Modern World*. He has published numerous articles, essays, and chapters. He is a judge for the National Jewish Book Awards, on the editorial boards for *Studies in the Shoah* and *Studies in American Jewish Literature*, and has lectured extensively on the Holocaust, Jewish literature, and theology both nationally and internationally.

PAUL BRAUNSTEIN ministered to Elie Wiesel when the latter was a UN reporter in New York in 1956. Wiesel was hit by a taxi, suffered forty-seven fractures and was refused admittance into one hospital because of lack of funds. Braunstein, a Catholic surgeon, called "Mr. Fracture" by admirers at Cornell Hospital, worked with Wiesel for months, and they became friends. Wiesel's novel, *The Accident*, is dedicated to Braunstein. A graduate of Harvard Medical School, Braunstein is currently Director of Surgery at Southside Hospital in Bay Shore, New York, Senior Surgeon at Good Samaritan Hospital in West Islip and Assistant Professor in Surgery at Stony Brook University. He published the first paper for the American Medical Association on seat belts.

LOUIS DANIEL BRODSKY was born in St. Louis, Missouri, in 1941, where he attended St. Louis Country Day School. After earning a B.A., magna cum laude, at Yale University in 1963, he received an M.A. in English from Washington University in 1967 and an M.A. in Creative Writing from San Francisco State University the following year. Mr. Brodsky has coedited eight scholarly books on Nobel laureate William Faulkner and authored a biography titled *William Faulkner, Life Glimpses*. His poems have appeared in *Harper's*, *Kansas Quarterly*, *Southern Review*, *Texas Quarterly*, and *National Forum*. He is the author of twenty volumes of poetry, five of which have been translated for French publication by Éditions Gallimard. In November 1993, Time Being Books will publish *The Capital Café: Poems of Redneck, U.S.A.*

HARRY JAMES CARGAS, in his twenty-fourth year at Webster University, St. Louis, has published twenty-six books, including *A Christian Response to the Holocaust* and *Conversations with Elie Wiesel*. He serves on many boards, including The National Christian Leadership Conference for Israel, International Philosophers for the Prevention of Nuclear Omnicide, Canine Assistance for the Disabled, the Catholic Institute for Holocaust Education and The Anne Frank Institute. He is the only Catholic appointed to the International Advisory Committee of *Yad Vashem*. For six years he served on the Executive Committee of the United States Holocaust Memorial Council.

BOB COSTAS, host of the late-night interview show, *LATER . . . with Bob Costas*, has worked with NBC since 1980. Known also for his enthusiastic sportscasting, Costas hosts *NFL LIVE*, co-hosted NBC's broadcast of 1988 Olympic Games from Seoul, Korea, and was the prime time host for the 1992 Barcelona Games. He has covered four World Series and hosted three Super Bowls for NBC. Costas has earned three American Sportscasters Awards. He has also been honored with Emmys four times and has been named National Sportscaster of the Year five times.

LEO EITINGER helped to operate on the young Elie Wiesel when both were prisoners in Auschwitz. Author of several textbooks and monographs on various topics in psychiatry, he is recognized as a world authority on special problems connected with refugees and concentration camp survivors. From 1950-1984 he served in the Psychiatric Department of the University Hospital in Oslo, Norway, where he became the Superintendent. A member of the Norwegian Academy of Sciences, he has earned many honors, including that of Commander of the Royal St. Olav.

EMIL L. FACKENHEIM was born in Halle, Germany. His theological and philosophical writings have been widely influential. After becoming a rabbi, he studied at the University of Aberdeen and earned a doctorate from The University of Toronto. A former Guggenheim Fellow and member of the Royal Society of Canada, he now lives and teaches in Israel. Among his books are *Metaphysics and Historicity*, *Quest for Past and Future*, *Encounters Between Judaism and Modern Philosophy*, *The Jewish Return to History*, and *God's Presence in History*. His work has been published in numerous academic journals in the United States, Canada, Germany and Israel.

GAIL M. GENDLER graduated cum laude from Syracuse University with a degree in Broadcast Journalism and is currently the Film Coordinator for *LATER . . . with Bob Costas* on NBC. In 1992, she received a nomination from the International Monitor Awards. Gendler is also recipient of the 1992 NATAS Sports Emmy for Outstanding Edited Sports Special for her work in Barcelona, Spain, during the games of the XXV Olympiad.

WILLIAM HEYEN's poems have appeared in more than a hundred periodicals, including *The New Yorker*, *Harper's*, *TriQuarterly*, *Poetry*, and *American Poetry Review*. His honors include two fellowships from the National Endowment for the Arts, the John Simon Guggenheim Fellowship in Poetry, the Eunice Tietjens Memorial Prize from *Poetry* magazine, and the Witter Bynner Prize for Poetry from the American Academy and Institute of Arts and Letters. Author of twelve books of poetry, his next, *The Host: Selected Poems 1965-1990*, will be published in 1994 by Time Being Books. Mr. Heyen is currently Professor of English and Poet in Residence at State University of New York College at Brockport.

FRANKLIN H. LITTELL has been called the "Father of Holocaust Studies in the United States." He is Emeritus Professor of Religion at Temple University and Adjunct Professor in the Institute of Contemporary Jewry at Hebrew University in Jerusalem. He chairs the Board of Trustees of the William O. Douglas Institute in Seattle and is Chairman of the Board of the Hamlin Institute in Philadelphia. He founded The Anne Frank Institute as well as the National Christian Leadership Conference for Israel. His many books include *The Crucifixion of the Jews*, *The Free Church*, and *From State Church to Pluralism*.

JOHN K. ROTH is currently a Professor of Philosophy and Chair of the Department of Philosophy and Religion at Claremont-McKenna College in Claremont, California. He received his M.A. and Ph.D. in philosophy from Yale University. Dr. Roth is the author and coauthor of numerous books on philosophy and religion. His most recent works are *Approaches to Auschwitz: The Holocaust and Its Legacy* (with Richard L. Rubenstein) and *The Questions of Philosophy* (with Frederick Sontag). Roth is currently on the Executive Committee of the Society for Social Philosophy and on the Editorial Board of the *American Journal of Theology and Philosophy*. He also served as the book review editor of *Holocaust and Genocide Studies*.

DOROTHEE SOELLE is a theologian who teaches in her native Germany as well as at Union Theological Seminary in New York. A poet, feminist and disarmament activist, Ms. Soelle is the author of *Choosing Life, Revolutionary Patience, Of War and Love, Beyond Mere Obedience, Political Theology, Suffering*, and *Death by Bread Alone*. She has earned graduate degrees from the University of Cologne and has taught philosophy, literature and religion at several German universities. In 1974 she was awarded the Theodore Heuss Medal for "civil courage and democracy," being the first theologian to earn that honor.

ELIE WIESEL, born on September 30, 1928, in Sighet, Romania, won the Nobel Peace Prize in 1986. He has also been nominated for the Nobel Prize for Literature. He is the Andrew Mellon Professor in the Humanities at Boston University, serves on thirty boards and has been awarded seventy-three honorary degrees in this country and abroad. His books have earned him two National Jewish Book Awards, two Jewish Heritage Awards for Literature, and the Prix Medicis and Prix Livre-Inter in France. His thirty-six volumes include *Night, Dawn, The Accident, The Jews of Silence, Souls on Fire, A Beggar in Jerusalem, The Fifth Son,* and *Twilight.*

Also available from **Time Being Books**

LOUIS DANIEL BRODSKY
You Can't Go Back, Exactly
The Thorough Earth
Four and Twenty Blackbirds Soaring
Mississippi Vistas: Volume One of *A Mississippi Trilogy*
Falling from Heaven: Holocaust Poems of a Jew and a Gentile
  (with William Heyen)
Forever, for Now: Poems for a Later Love
Mistress Mississippi: Volume Three of *A Mississippi Trilogy*
A Gleam in the Eye: Poems for a First Baby
Gestapo Crows: Holocaust Poems
The Capital Café: Poems of Redneck, U.S.A.

ROBERT HAMBLIN
From the Ground Up: Poems of One Southerner's Passage to Adulthood

WILLIAM HEYEN
Falling from Heaven: Holocaust Poems of a Jew and a Gentile
  (with Louis Daniel Brodsky)
Erika: Poems of the Holocaust
Pterodactyl Rose: Poems of Ecology
Ribbons: The Gulf War — A Poem

TED HIRSCHFIELD
German Requiem: Poems of the War and the Atonement of a Third
  Reich Child

VIRGINIA V. JAMES HLAVSA
Waking October Leaves: Reanimations of a Small-Town Girl

RODGER KAMENETZ
The Missing Jew: New and Selected Poems

NORBERT KRAPF
Somewhere in Southern Indiana: Poems of Midwestern Origins

JOSEPH MEREDITH
Hunter's Moon: Poems from Boyhood to Manhood

FOR OUR FREE CATALOG OR TO ORDER

(800) 331-6605
Monday through Friday, 8 a.m. to 4 p.m. Central time
FAX: (314) 432-7939

DEMCO